T0386286

CUISINES OF THE MULTIVERSE

THE OFFICIAL COOKBOOK

MAGIC
THE GATHERING

CUISINES OF THE MULTIVERSE
THE OFFICIAL COOKBOOK

Recipes & Photography by **VICTORIA ROSENTHAL**

Text by **JENNA HELLAND**

**TITAN
BOOKS**

London

An Insight Editions Book

CONTENTS

INTRODUCTION

Teferi surveyed his kitchen. His friends would arrive in an hour, and he still had three hours of work left to do. He cast a small spell to slow time down so he could breathe easily and finish the preparations without rushing. He was serving Zhalfirin Grilled Flank Steak as his main dish, and as his father had taught him, great things take time and patience.

When he was a child, his father tried to teach him how to cook, but Teferi struggled to stay in the moment. There was always a new, youthful adventure to rush to, and he couldn't be bothered to spend hours preparing a meal. Oh, how he had changed since then. He hoped his father knew that he had been listening, even if it didn't seem like he was. He hoped he had become like his father, a patient and compassionate man who appreciated the wisdom of others.

As he prepared the vegetables for his Heart of Yavimaya salad, he reminisced about an evening in a Kessig village. He was in a vegetable patch looking for ingredients to make a tasty stew. The garden was bursting with brightly colored pumpkins, squash, and other vegetables not unlike those that grew on Dominaria. One of them looked exactly like an artichoke, although it was called the "Last Heartbeat of the Dying Cathar," or some other gothic, macabre mouthful.

Teferi took an artichoke from his counter and inspected it in the afternoon light. The geometrical pattern was mathematically perfect—a brilliant design for such a succulent food. His mind was flooded with all the times he'd seen artichokes on different worlds: in the window-box gardens of Ravnica; growing wild in the Turntimber on Zendikar; in a plot behind the Strixhaven dining hall. He had walked on hundreds of planes, each distinct from the others. No two skies were the same. Unique architecture shaped by wondrously different minds and hands. Each animal, creature, and monster had distinctiveness shaped by the lands they lived in. There were many occasions when Teferi was awestruck at the differences between worlds, but he'd never considered what made them alike.

Teferi picked up an apple and paced the kitchen, deep in thought. Throughout the vast Multiverse, each plane had distinct conflicts, stories, and magic. If there was one thing that was constant, it was the need for sustenance. Food was an essential way of bringing families and communities together, no matter where they were from. Denizens in every village, guildhall, castle, and floating city in the Multiverse gathered ingredients, cooked according to their customs, and sat together in fellowship to nourish their bodies. Such culinary details might be hidden behind the disputes and strife, but they were important just the same.

Teferi set his apple down. He'd been crunching on it for a while, but thanks to his spell, it was only half eaten. Somewhere, across some other distant plane, someone else was cooking for their friends too. With all that he'd seen and done, there was still much to learn. Maybe someday, he should write a book: *Cuisines of the Multiverse*. Or maybe, somebody already had. He smiled to himself with warmth in his heart and continued cutting the vegetables.

RAVNICA

Ravnica is a sprawling metropolis that covers the entire plane. Everything revolves around its ten guilds, each unique in its identity and purpose. Ravnica has weathered many crises over its long history. Recently, the city triumphed over the evil dragon Nicol Bolas in a devastating war. The Guildpact—the magical basis for law and moderation between the guilds to maintain peace—emerged from these tumultuous events intact. No matter what catastrophes befall them, the denizens of Ravnica endure.

Krenko, goblin mob boss and thief extraordinaire, had always loved his home. He adored strolling down the Transguild Promenade where creatures from all guilds walked together. Grabbing a coffee from the stand near Vizkopa Bank and watching the crowds for an easy mark was often the highlight of his day. He loved the smell of funnel cake wafting from the bakeries at the edge of the Gruul lands. There was something for everyone in this wondrous city.

Krenko knew Ravnica better than anyone, particularly the Tenth District. He'd been inside every guildhall, Undercity tunnel, and carnarium for miles around—and he'd pilfered something from each one. But ever since the war with the dragon, Krenko had been considering retirement. Maybe it was time for him to leave the exciting life of petty crime and build a little cabin somewhere out in the Gruul lands.

An invitation from the most unexpected source quickly changed his mind (at least, for the time being). Jace Beleren, former Living Guildpact and a legend to many across Ravnica, wanted Krenko to find a recipe that embodied each guild. Jace offered an absurd amount of zinos for this easy job. Krenko couldn't say no; there might even be cake along the walk. After days of harder work than he expected, Krenko completed his task. It was time to meet with the mind mage, hand over the goods, and collect his fee.

BELEREN'S BLEND

Difficulty: ■■■□□ • **Prep Time:** 45 minutes • **Inactive Time:** 2 hours • **Cook Time:** 1 hour

Yield: 1 drink • **Dietary Notes:** Vegetarian, Gluten-Free

Jace's home was just what Krenko expected: arcane tomes on every surface and stealable things on every shelf. Krenko was eyeing an alluring orb when Jace appeared with two mugs of coffee topped with a mysterious foam. As Krenko sipped appreciatively, Jace described how he made his favorite drink. A Bird of Paradise egg was ideal, but any egg would do. He told Krenko that Beleren's Blend inspired this task. It was more than a drink—it embodied his feelings about Ravnica. If a cup of coffee could reveal how he felt about Ravnica, perhaps food from the guilds could unveil the same? Krenko took one last gulp and began his report.

Butterfly Pea Sweetened Condensed Milk

2 cups whole milk

¾ cup sugar

pinch of salt

10 butterfly pea flowers

1 teaspoon vanilla paste

Egg Coffee

2 egg yolks

3 to 4 tablespoons butterfly pea sweetened condensed milk OR 3 to 4 tablespoons sweetened condensed milk

1 drop blue food dye, optional

20 g robusta coffee

300 g water

Note: *Consuming raw eggs can increase your risk of foodborne illnesses. Pasteurized eggs should be used for this.*

Combine milk, sugar, salt, and butterfly pea flowers in a saucepan. Heat over medium-high heat and bring to a simmer. Reduce the heat and allow to simmer for 40 to 50 minutes, or until reduced by half and thickened. Make sure to whisk occasionally to avoid any sticking to the bottom of the pan. Remove and discard the butterfly pea flowers.

Remove from the heat and whisk in the vanilla paste. Transfer to an airtight container and allow to cool completely. Once cooled, cover and place in the refrigerator for at least 2 hours before serving. Can be stored in the refrigerator for up to 3 weeks.

Place the egg yolks and butterfly pea sweetened condensed milk (or sweetened condensed milk and blue food dye) in a medium bowl. Using a hand mixer, whip until it becomes thick and doubled in size, about 4 to 5 minutes.

Make one serving of coffee with robusta beans, using the given ratio of coffee to water, and your preferred method. Alternatively, substitute with a strong cup of coffee or two shots of espresso.

Transfer two-thirds of the coffee to a cup. Place the cup in a bowl with hot water to keep the coffee hot. Carefully top with the whipped egg mixture. Pour the remaining third of the coffee over the egg mixture and leave in the bowl for 60 seconds. Remove the cup and serve.

AZOR'S SEALS

Difficulty: ■■■□□ • **Prep Time:** 45 minutes • **Inactive Time:** 2 hours • **Cook Time:** 30 minutes
Yield: 12 rolls • **Dietary Notes:** Vegetarian

Krenko strolled into Azorius headquarters like he didn't have a rap sheet a mile long. New Prahv was the seat of law and order on Ravnica. Countless scribes were working hard to craft, maintain, and enforce the laws from here. It was not a place Krenko wanted to linger in for long. The scent of baked goods led him to an unassuming break room where he found a plate of delicious breakfast pastries. A friendly lawmage told him the history of this iconic Azorius dish between bites: Azor was a sphinx planeswalker who wrote most of the original Guildpact, and these were his favorite food. Some claim the pastry was the inspiration for the Azorius symbol.

Dough

¾ cup milk, warmed (100°F)

2 ¼ teaspoons active
  dry yeast

3 ½ cups all-purpose flour

⅓ cup sugar

1 teaspoon kosher salt

3 egg yolks

2 teaspoons vanilla paste

½ cup unsalted butter,
  melted and cooled

Cream Cheese Filling

8 ounces cream cheese, room
  temperature

¼ cup powdered sugar

1 teaspoon vanilla extract

1 egg yolk

½ teaspoon salt

Poppy Seed Filling

½ cup poppy seeds

¼ cup milk

3 tablespoons apricot jam

pinch of salt

½ teaspoon vanilla paste

Egg Wash

1 egg yolk

2 tablespoons milk

Combine the milk and yeast. Allow the yeast to bloom, about 5 minutes. Combine the flour, sugar, and salt in a large bowl. Add the yeast mixture, egg yolks, and vanilla paste. Mix until it just comes together.

Add the butter and mix until a dough forms. If the dough is too sticky, add 1 tablespoon of flour at a time. If it is too dry, add 1 tablespoon of milk at a time. Knead the dough for 5 minutes. Transfer to an oiled bowl, cover, and let rest for 2 hours or until it has doubled in size.

While the dough is resting, take the time to make the two fillings. For the cream cheese filling, whisk together the cream cheese, sugar, egg yolk, vanilla extract, and salt in a medium bowl until smooth. Set aside.

For the poppy seed filling, place the poppy seeds in a food processor (or mortar and pestle) and grind into a paste. Transfer to a small pan and add the remaining ingredients. Place over medium-low heat and cook until a thick paste forms. Remove from the heat and allow to cool completely, then transfer to a pastry bag.

Once the dough has doubled, punch down and lightly knead. Prepare 2 baking sheets with parchment paper. Divide the dough into 12 equal portions. Shape into round balls, lightly press down to flatten slightly, and place on the baking sheet. Cover with plastic wrap and let rest for 30 minutes or until doubled in size.

Note: *Make sure to leave enough space so they don't touch when they expand.*

Preheat oven to 350°F. Press down and make a large indent in the center of each of the rolls. Whisk the egg yolk and milk for the egg wash. Brush each of the indented rolls.

For half of the rolls, fill the bottom with the cream cheese filling. Take the poppy seed filling and carefully draw on the Azorius Senate logo. With the other half, fill the bottom with the poppy seed filling and top with a dollop of cream cheese filling.

Place in the oven and bake for 20 to 25 minutes or until the dough is golden brown and the filling is set.

Keyhole Cake

Difficulty: ■■■□ • **Prep Time:** 45 minutes • **Inactive Time:** 1 ½ hours • **Cook Time:** 30 minutes
Yield: 4 cakes • **Dietary Notes:** Vegetarian

Krenko crept through the dark tunnel toward the glow of candlelight and an ominous figure. The Dimir legend had many names and many faces, but to Krenko, he would always be Mr. Taz. They'd made this rendezvous before, and each time Krenko never knew what to expect. Over the years, the secretive Mr. Taz had given him a broken sword, a stolen emerald, a cursed manuscript, and other suspicious items. Today, it was cake! Mr. Taz had spent all afternoon baking the Dimir's signature recipe, the Keyhole Cake. Created by Szadek and perfected by Etrata, Mr. Taz believed it was time for the Dimir's baking brilliance to emerge from the shadows. After taking a bite, Krenko immediately agreed.

Caramel Filling

⅓ cup heavy cream

1 teaspoon vanilla extract

½ cup sugar

2 tablespoons corn syrup

1 ½ tablespoons water

2 tablespoons unsalted butter, cold

¾ teaspoon kosher salt

flaky salt

Caramel Filling

Prepare a 9-by-5-inch baking pan with aluminum foil. Place a layer of parchment paper on top. Spray with nonstick spray and set aside.

Place the heavy cream and vanilla extract in a small saucepan. Heat until just before a simmer. Remove from the heat and set aside.

Mix the sugar, corn syrup, and water together in a tall saucepan. Place over medium heat. Heat until the sugar becomes a liquid and turns into a deep amber color (or reaches 300°F), about 8 to 10 minutes.

Note: *It is important that you do not stir this mixture until mentioned. Otherwise, the sugar will crystallize, and you will have to start all over again. You can lightly swirl the pan, but do not whisk or stir with a spatula.*

Remove the pan from the heat and slowly add the warmed heavy cream while whisking. Keep in mind the mixture will bubble and triple in size. Keep whisking. Return to the heat and cook until it reaches 250°F, about 3 to 5 minutes.

Turn off the heat and add the butter and kosher salt. Whisk until it stops bubbling. Transfer to the prepared baking pan. Lightly tap the pan on a surface to remove any large air bubbles. Sprinkle the top with flaky salt. Let rest at room temperature for 1 hour.

Remove the caramel and transfer to a cutting board. Using a 1½-inch round cookie cutter, cut 8 caramel discs. Transfer to a plate with a piece of parchment paper. Place in the freezer for 20 minutes, up to 1 hour.

Note: *There will be a bit of extra caramel after you cut out the pieces you need. Enjoy it for all your hard work!*

Continued on next page

Cake

5 ounces dark chocolate

⅓ cup unsalted butter,
additional for the ramekins

¼ cup all-purpose flour

1 teaspoon instant coffee powder

¼ teaspoon kosher salt

2 whole eggs

2 egg yolks

¼ cup sugar

2 teaspoons vanilla extract

Cake

Combine the chocolate and butter in a medium saucepan and heat over medium-low heat. Cook until the chocolate is melted. Set aside to cool completely.

Preheat oven to 375°F. Prepare four 6-ounce ramekins by generously rubbing the insides with butter. Combine the flour, instant coffee powder, and salt in a small bowl.

Whisk the whole eggs, egg yolks, and white sugar in a large bowl until pale and thickened. Whisk in the cooled chocolate and vanilla extract. Fold in the flour mixture until just combined.

Fill each of the ramekins just under halfway with the batter. Place 2 of the frozen caramel discs in the center of each of the ramekins. Cover with the remaining batter.

Transfer the ramekins onto a baking sheet. Bake for 15 to 17 minutes or until the cake is cooked through. Let cool for 2 minutes. Run a knife on the side of the ramekin and invert on a plate to remove.

Note: *Be careful: The caramel in the center will be very hot!*

DEMON DELIGHTS

Difficulty: ■■■□□ • **Prep Time:** 30 minutes • **Inactive Time:** 30 minutes • **Cook Time:** 2 - 4 minutes per batch
Yield: 10 - 12 mini funnel cakes • **Dietary Notes:** Vegetarian

Tied to a spinning wooden wheel with knives hurtling toward him, Krenko thought about his life choices. Why had he become a thief? Why hadn't he stolen that orb in Jace's apartment? And why had he agreed to this fiasco for the sake of a recipe? As he whirled around, he heard the carnival music. Tightrope-walkers came into view with their flaming hoops, and the roustabouts were whipping the crowd into a frenzy. In the colorful, chaotic blur, Rakdos's particular flavor of fun suddenly made sense. Soon, his new friends cut him down and sent him on his way with a bag of Demon Delights, compliments of Rakdos the Demon himself.

Cardamom Topping

2 tablespoons powdered sugar

1 tablespoon light brown sugar

½ teaspoon cardamom

½ teaspoon cinnamon

Taro Topping

2 tablespoons powdered sugar

½ tablespoon taro powder

Spicy Cocoa Topping

2 tablespoons powdered sugar

½ tablespoon cocoa powder

½ teaspoon cayenne pepper

¼ teaspoon cinnamon

Note: *For a bit of chaos, you can increase the amount of cayenne pepper to bring some fiery excitement.*

Funnel Cake

2 eggs

1 cup milk

1 teaspoon vanilla extract

2 cups all-purpose flour

3 tablespoons sugar

1 teaspoon baking powder

1 teaspoon kosher salt

peanut oil for frying

Combine each of the topping combinations in separate airtight containers. These can be stored at room temperature for up to 3 weeks.

To make the funnel cake batter, whisk together the eggs, milk, and vanilla extract. Add the flour, sugar, baking powder, and salt and whisk until it comes together. Transfer the batter into large pastry bags. Allow to rest at room temperature for 30 minutes.

Place 2 inches of peanut oil in a deep pot and heat to 360°F. Once heated, cut the bottom of the pastry bag and drizzle the batter into the hot oil, creating a 4-inch-wide funnel cake.

Note: *The batter will sink to the bottom but should rise to the top quickly as it cooks.*

Allow to fry for 1 to 2 minutes, until the bottom is golden brown. Flip and cook for another 1 to 2 minutes, until that side is golden brown. Remove from the oil and transfer to a plate lined with a paper towel to drain. Repeat with the remaining batter.

Top each funnel cake with the topping of your choice.

Gruulash

Difficulty: ■■■□□ • **Prep Time:** 45 minutes • **Cook Time:** 3 hours
Yield: 4 - 6 servings • **Dietary Notes:** Dairy-Free, Gluten-Free

All hail Ilharg, Bringer of the End-Raze! Krenko shouted those praises along with the rest of the Gruul. They were celebrating the boar-god who would one day bring an end to all civilization. Krenko felt an affinity for the Gruul. The lawlessness and freedom their clans valued appealed to him. And they were always happy to share their mouth-watering Gruulash, which was tastier than anything he'd ever had in a restaurant. Krenko enjoyed the meal by the warmth of the bonfire under an open sky, feeling full and invigorated, but he also appreciated the return to the city streets and indoor plumbing.

Marinade

1 ½ lbs wild boar

2 thyme stalks

1 rosemary sprig

3 garlic cloves, crushed

1 cinnamon stick

1 tablespoon black peppercorns

One 750-milliliter bottle red wine

Gruulash

4 slices bacon, sliced

1 ½ lbs marinated wild boar meat

1 onion, sliced

½ red onion, sliced

kosher salt

4 garlic cloves, chopped

3 celery stalks, chopped

2 carrots, cut into large chunks

2 cups reserved red wine

One 15-ounce can diced tomatoes

6 ounces tomato paste

1 tablespoon sweet paprika

1 teaspoon coriander

1 teaspoon cumin

2 teaspoons caraway seeds

10 juniper berries, crushed

2 cups beef stock

2 bay leaves

4 white potatoes, peeled and cut
    into large chunks

Marinade

Combine everything in an airtight container. Refrigerate for at least 24 hours to help pull out some of the gamey flavor from the meat.

The next day, strain everything through a fine mesh strainer. Reserve 2 cups of the wine. Remove the wild boar from all the spices. Discard everything but the boar meat and the reserved wine.

Gruulash

Heat a medium dutch oven over medium-high heat. Add the bacon and cook until crispy, about 8 minutes. Transfer the bacon to a plate but leave the fat in the dutch oven.

Add a single layer of the wild boar but be careful not to overcrowd the dutch oven. Brown all sides of the meat. Remove and place on the plate with the bacon. Add canola oil, if needed, and continue this process until all the boar has been browned.

Add the white and red onions. Season generously with salt. Cook until the onion is softened and has browned slightly, about 10 minutes.

Add the garlic, celery, and carrots and cook for another 2 minutes. Pour in the red wine and bring to a boil. Allow to simmer for 5 minutes, until it reduces by one-fourth. Add the diced tomatoes and tomato paste and mix until well combined.

Add the bacon and wild boar meat back to the dutch oven and stir together. Sprinkle the paprika, coriander, cumin, caraway seeds, and juniper berries over the meat. Toss until well coated.

Add the beef stock. Mix until everything is well combined. Add the bay leaves. Bring to a boil and then reduce the heat to low. Allow to simmer for 2 hours, or until the boar is tender.

Add the potato and cook for another 45 minutes, or until the potatoes are firm but tender.

Trostani's Three Bean Salad

Difficulty: ■□□□□ • **Prep Time:** 15 minutes • **Inactive Time:** 30 minutes • **Yield:** 6 servings
Dietary Notes: Vegetarian, Gluten-Free

Krenko marched up to recruitment agents outside of Vitu-Ghazi and told them he wanted to join the Conclave. Twenty minutes later, he was at the evening ceremony dressed in white and holding a bowl of beans. All Selesnyans helped make dinner, and tonight, they were making Trostani's personal favorite. Both the guildmaster and the salad were a combo of three components representing life, order, and harmony. Melodic chanting accompanied the preparations; soon everyone was singing and swaying. Even Krenko felt his toes a-tapping. It was the most joyful salad-making he'd ever had the privilege of witnessing. After dinner, he snuck out, guildless but grinning ear to pointed ear.

Dressing

¼ cup olive oil

zest and juice of 3 limes

1 tablespoon honey

3 garlic cloves, minced

1 teaspoon ground cumin

½ teaspoon ground coriander

¼ teaspoon chili powder

1 teaspoon kosher salt

½ teaspoon ground black pepper

Salad

One 15-ounce can kidney beans,
   strained and washed

One 15-ounce can black beans,
   strained and washed

One 15-ounce can pinto beans,
   strained and washed

1 shallot, sliced

1 bunch cilantro, minced

1 cucumber, peeled, seeds removed,
   and chopped

Whisk together all the ingredients for the dressing in a small bowl.

Place the beans, shallot, cilantro, and cucumber in a large bowl. Lightly toss to mix. Add the dressing and toss until combined. Allow to rest for at least 30 minutes in the refrigerator before serving.

Orzhov's Splendor

Difficulty: ■■■□□ • **Prep Time:** 30 minutes • **Inactive Time:** 1 ½ hours • **Cook Time:** 1 hour
Yield: 1 tomahawk steak • **Dietary Notes:** Gluten-Free

Kaya and Krenko sat on silk cushions in the Orzhov Guildhall's dusty attic, stuffing themselves with luxurious food swiped from the banquet hall a few floors below them. Kaya was amused by Krenko's mission and happily shared the dish that was so good, it almost made her want to remain guildmaster. But, in the end, Kaya wasn't swayed by the lavishness and decadence of the guild. She'd rather hunt monsters, banish specters, or help her friends than contend with the Church of Deals. Dropping in for an occasional visit was the perfect compromise. Kaya and Krenko sat together long into the night, swapping ghost stories and enjoying Orzhov's Splendor.

Steak

One 3-inch-thick tomahawk steak

kosher salt

crushed black pepper

Poivre Sauce

2 tablespoons unsalted butter

1 shallot, minced

2 tablespoons brandy

2 tablespoons brined green peppercorns

1 teaspoon ground black pepper

1 cup beef stock

¼ cup heavy cream

Steak

An hour before you are going to start cooking the steak, prepare a baking sheet with aluminum foil and top with a wire rack. Remove the steak from the refrigerator and generously season with salt and pepper. Place on the wire rack and let it sit at room temperature for 1 hour.

Note: *You want to make sure you thoroughly season the steak. As it rests, the salt will penetrate into the meat and season all of it. If you have a food probe thermometer, place it in the steak to keep an eye on the internal temperature as it cooks.*

Preheat oven to 250°F. Place the steak in the oven and cook until it reaches an internal temperature of 120°F, about 45 minutes to 1 hour.

Heat a large cast-iron skillet over high heat. Once heated, add the steak, and cook until it forms a golden, dark crust, about 2 to 3 minutes. Flip and sear the other side the same way. Remove from the skillet and wrap in aluminum foil. Let rest for 15 minutes before cutting.

Poivre Sauce

Using the same skillet that was used to sear the steak, place over medium-high heat. Add the butter and melt. Add the shallot and cook until softened, about 2 minutes.

Turn off the heat and add the brandy. Turn the heat back on to medium-high and cook until the liquid has reduced by half, about 30 seconds to 1 minute.

Note: *We turn off the heat here to make sure the alcohol does not start a fire.*

Add the green peppercorns and ground pepper and stir for about 30 seconds. Stir in the beef stock and heavy cream. Reduce the heat to medium and allow to simmer until thickened, about 3 to 5 minutes.

NIV-FIZZIT

Difficulty: ■□□□□ • **Prep Time:** 15 minutes • **Cook Time:** 45 minutes
Yield: 12 - 16 servings • **Dietary Notes:** Vegan, Gluten-Free

After eyeing the high-tech defenses of Nivix, Krenko decided to try another approach: through the pub. The Electrosizzler was a well-known Izzet hangout, and Krenko found a stool at the bar, hoping to run into one. He turned to the man next to him and asked him for recommendations. As luck would have it, the man was none other than Ral Zarek, the famous leader of the guild. Ral was happy to share the finest Izzet cuisine in the house. Over the course of an enjoyable evening, the two ate their way through everything from Chemister Chips to Overloaded Nachos. But it was Ral's favorite drink, which he had created in honor of his mentor Niv-Mizzet, that earned a spot in Krenko's recipe roster.

Ginger Syrup

1 cup water

1 cup sugar

2 strips lemon peel

1 strip lime peel

One 4-inch piece of ginger, sliced

Per Cocktail

2 ounces gin

1 ounce ginger syrup

1 ounce lemon juice

½ ounce lime juice

½ cup ginger beer

ice

2 lemon slices

2 buzz buttons

Ginger Syrup

Combine all the ingredients in a saucepan and place over medium-high heat. Whisk until the sugar has dissolved and then bring to a boil. Reduce the heat and simmer for 45 minutes. Remove from the heat and strain into an airtight container. Once cooled, cover, and store in the refrigerator for up to 2 weeks.

Per Cocktail

Fill a cocktail shaker with ice. Add gin, ginger syrup, lemon juice, and lime juice. Shake thoroughly for 15 seconds. Pour through a mesh strainer into a highball glass with fresh ice cubes.

Fill the glass with ginger beer until topped off. Top with lemon slices and buzz buttons.

VRASKA'S UNDERCITY BRUSCHETTA

Difficulty: ■■□□□ • **Prep Time:** 1 hour • **Cook Time:** 20 minutes • **Yield:** 20 portions • **Dietary Notes:** Vegetarian

Krenko's timing was perfect! The annual Mushroom Festival was in full swing in the Undercity. He passed under a banner reading: Mushrooms: Food, Fashion, and Fun. He paused to cheer on the shamblers in the Portobello Relay Race and then listened intently as the Golgari engineers debuted the latest in shroom recycling systems. Finally, he reached the restaurant he'd been seeking: The Gorgon and the Gorgonzola. Run by devotees of the planeswalker Vraska, these accomplished chefs celebrate everything she has done for the Swarm. When he asked them for a dish that most embodied their guild, they presented him with a plate of bruschetta named in honor of their queen.

6 ounces gorgonzola

8 ounces mascarpone, room temperature

3 ounces goat cheese

12 baby portobello mushrooms, stems discarded and sliced

12 shiitake mushrooms, stems discarded and sliced

1 ounce porcini mushrooms, rehydrated and sliced

5 garlic cloves, sliced

2 teaspoons dried thyme

kosher salt

ground black pepper

Twenty 1-inch-thick baguette slices

olive oil

balsamic vinegar

Place the gorgonzola, mascarpone, and goat cheese in a food processor and blend until smooth.

Heat a medium pan over medium-high heat. Add olive oil. Add the baby portobello, shiitake, and porcini mushroooms, and cook until they have turned golden brown, about 10 to 15 minutes.

Add the garlic and thyme. Cook until the garlic has browned slightly, about 5 minutes. Season with salt and pepper.

Place the baguette slices on a baking sheet and bake for 4 minutes at 400°F. Flip and bake for another 4 minutes. Once baked, take each of the baked slices and brush olive oil over them. Top with the cheese mixture and mushrooms. Drizzle each with balsamic vinegar.

Boros Legion Rations

Difficulty: ■■□□□ • **Prep Time:** 1 hour • **Inactive Time:** 24 hours • **Cook Time:** 5 hours
Yield: 6 - 8 servings • **Dietary Notes:** N/A

Krenko brushed off his old Boros uniform and joined the new recruits for the day's drills. While Battleforce angels flew overhead shouting words of encouragement, soldiers marched up and down the One-Hundred Steps, the gateway into the Tenth District. After his legs started to ache, Krenko had enough and went to chat with the mess sergeant preparing lunch for the soldiers. When asked to describe Boros cuisine, the chef told Krenko that each soldier must be well-fed so they can be ready to protect the people of their great city. Then he handed Krenko a red-and-white box filled with hearty fare and told him to get back to training.

Jerky

½ cup soy sauce

½ cup honey

¼ cup worcestershire sauce

1 teaspoon liquid smoke

2 tablespoons garlic powder

1 tablespoon onion powder

2 tablespoons ground black pepper

2 lbs top round roast, thinly sliced

Nut Bar

1 cup almonds

1 cup cashews

1 cup walnuts

1 cup pistachios

¼ cup dried cherries

¼ cup white sesame seeds

2 teaspoons kosher salt

1 teaspoon ground cardamom

½ cup honey

¼ cup maple syrup

Jerky

Combine the soy sauce, honey, worcestershire sauce, liquid smoke, garlic powder, onion powder, and pepper in a gallon-sized sealable bag. Add the thinly sliced beef, seal, and shake until the beef is covered in the marinade. Place in the refrigerator overnight to marinate, up to 24 hours.

Preheat oven to 175°F. Prepare a baking sheet with aluminum foil, place a wire rack on top, and spray with nonstick spray. Take the beef out of the marinade and let excess liquid drip off. Place on the wire rack.

Cook in the oven for 4 to 5 hours, or until the beef is dry and chewy. Let cool completely. Store in an airtight container in the refrigerator for up to 1 week.

Nut Bar

Place the almonds, cashews, walnuts, and pistachios in a food processor. Pulse until the nuts are completely crumbled. Add the rest of the ingredients and blend until completely combined.

Line an 8-by-8-inch deep baking sheet with parchment paper. Spread the mixture into the baking sheet and flatten. Cover with a layer of parchment paper.

Note: *You can add an extra layer of crushed nuts on top to give the bars an additional texture profile. Lightly press the nuts on before covering with the parchment paper.*

Place in the refrigerator and allow to rest for 24 hours. Remove from the baking sheet and cut into 1½-by-1-inch pieces. Can be stored in an airtight container in the refrigerator for up to 2 weeks.

Continued on next page

Trail Mix

One 15-ounce can chickpeas, rinsed and dried

1 tablespoon olive oil

1 ½ teaspoons kosher salt

1 teaspoon cumin

1 ½ teaspoons turmeric

½ teaspoon chili powder

¾ cup cashews

½ cup raw almonds

½ cup raw macadamia nuts

½ cup raw pumpkin seeds

½ teaspoon ground ginger

¼ teaspoon garlic powder

¼ teaspoon cayenne pepper

3 ounces dried mango, chopped

¾ cup yogurt-covered raisins

Hard-Boiled Quail Eggs

12 quail eggs

Trail Mix

Preheat oven to 425°F. Combine the chickpeas, olive oil, ½ teaspoon salt, cumin, ½ teaspoon turmeric, and chili powder in a bowl. Toss until coated. Transfer to a baking sheet lined with parchment paper. Bake for 30 minutes, shaking the pan every 10 minutes to turn the chickpeas. Set aside to cool completely.

Reduce the heat of the oven to 350°F. Place the cashews, almonds, macadamia nuts, and pumpkin seeds on a baking sheet lined with parchment paper. Bake for 8 to 10 minutes, or until the nuts are lightly toasted. Set aside to cool completely.

Once the chickpeas and nuts have cooled, place in a bowl and add 1 teaspoon salt, 1 teaspoon turmeric, ground ginger, garlic powder, and cayenne pepper. Toss to coat completely. Add the mango and yogurt-covered raisins. Can be stored in an airtight container at room temperature for up to 1 week.

Hard-Boiled Quail Eggs

Bring a pot of water to a boil. Gently place the eggs in the pot, cover, and cook for 3 ½ minutes. Once cooked, immediately take the pot off the stove and place under cold running water. Carefully remove the shells from the eggs. Can be stored in an airtight container in the refrigerator for up to 3 days.

Krasis Fusion Boil

Difficulty: ■■■□□ • **Prep Time:** 45 minutes • **Cook Time:** 1 ½ hours • **Yield:** 4 - 6 servings • **Dietary Notes:** Shellfish

At the Simic Guildhall, Krenko witnessed science and magic working in tandem. The biomancers were preparing a nutritional supplement at the end of a particularly grueling research cycle. Speaker Vannifar praised the group for their recent creation, a jellyfish-hydra-beast-ooze-snake hybrid! The first of its kind! The biomancers raised their glasses and toasted each other with shouts of: Graft! Evolve! Adapt! As the steaming bowls were passed around, everyone debated what to name their new creation, and they settled on "Kraj Junior." Krenko smiled at his soup, and it smiled back. Simic creations were part experiment, part alchemy, and all delicious.

Spice Mix

- 3 tablespoons smoked paprika
- 1 tablespoon cayenne
- 1 tablespoon kosher salt
- 1 tablespoon ground black pepper
- 2 teaspoons sugar
- 2 teaspoons ground celery seeds
- 2 teaspoons mustard powder
- 2 teaspoons garlic powder
- 1 teaspoon bay leaf powder
- 1 teaspoon coriander
- 1 teaspoon dried thyme
- 1 teaspoon dried oregano
- 1 teaspoon ground ginger
- ½ teaspoon ground mace
- ¼ teaspoon ground nutmeg
- ¼ teaspoon ground allspice
- ¼ teaspoon ground cinnamon
- ⅛ teaspoon ground cloves

Garlic Butter

- 1 ½ cups unsalted butter
- 25 garlic cloves, minced
- ¼ cup of spice mix
- juice of 1 lemon
- 1 tablespoon paprika
- 1 teaspoon ground black pepper

Boil

- ⅓ cup spice mix
- One 4-inch piece of ginger, sliced
- 3 lemongrass stalks
- 1 onion, quartered
- 1 lemon, sliced
- 2 heads of garlic, cut in half
- 2 bay leaves
- ¼ cup fish sauce
- 12 cups water
- 1 lb red potatoes
- 1 lb smoked sausage
- 2 lbs large shrimp, heads on and deveined
- 2 lbs crab legs
- 3 ears of corn, cut in half

Spice Mix

Combine all the ingredients for the spice mix.

Garlic Butter

Place the butter in a saucepan over medium-high heat. Cook until the butter has melted completely. Add the garlic and cook for 10 minutes, until the garlic is very fragrant and softened.

Add the spice mix, lemon juice, paprika, and black pepper. Remove from the heat and set aside. Before tossing in with the seafood, warm up slightly.

Boil

Combine the spice mix, ginger, lemongrass, onion, lemon, garlic, bay leaves, fish sauce, and water in a large pot. Place over medium-high heat and bring to a boil. Reduce the heat and simmer for 40 minutes.

Add the potatoes and cook for 15 minutes. Add the sausage and cook for 10 minutes. Add the shrimp, crab legs, and corn and cook until the shrimp is cooked through, about 3 to 5 minutes.

Note: *If the pot is too small, you might have to cook the shrimp, crab, and corn in batches. Make sure to not overcook the potatoes.*

Strain everything and transfer the potatoes, sausage, shrimp, crab, and corn into a large bowl, discarding the other ingredients. Toss and mix with the garlic butter.

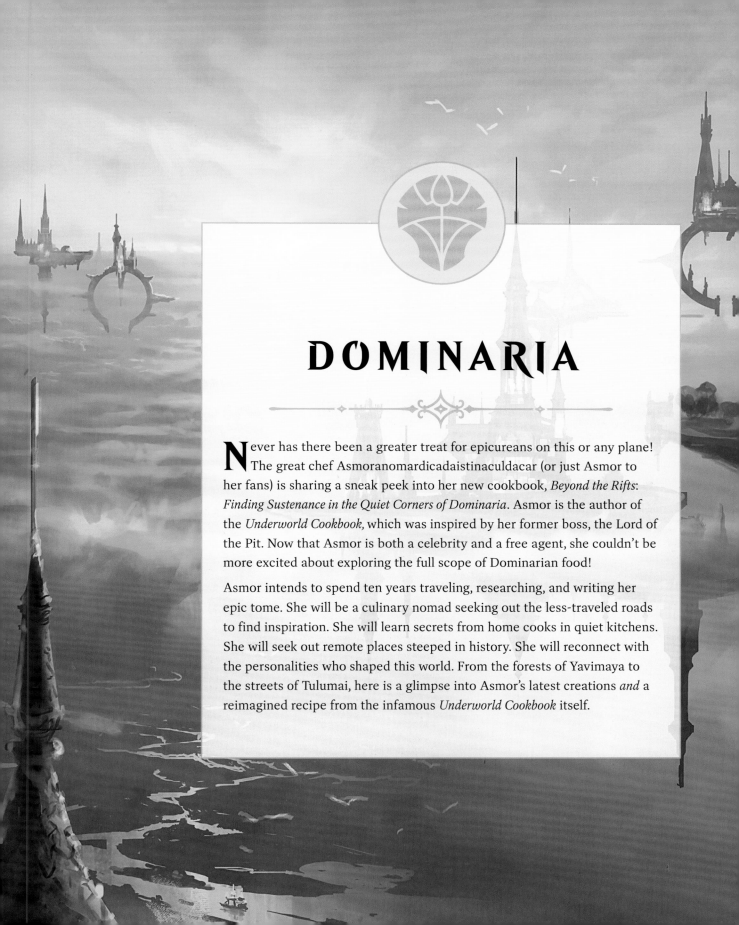

DOMINARIA

Never has there been a greater treat for epicureans on this or any plane! The great chef Asmoranomardicadaistinaculdacar (or just Asmor to her fans) is sharing a sneak peek into her new cookbook, *Beyond the Rifts*: *Finding Sustenance in the Quiet Corners of Dominaria*. Asmor is the author of the *Underworld Cookbook,* which was inspired by her former boss, the Lord of the Pit. Now that Asmor is both a celebrity and a free agent, she couldn't be more excited about exploring the full scope of Dominarian food!

Asmor intends to spend ten years traveling, researching, and writing her epic tome. She will be a culinary nomad seeking out the less-traveled roads to find inspiration. She will learn secrets from home cooks in quiet kitchens. She will seek out remote places steeped in history. She will reconnect with the personalities who shaped this world. From the forests of Yavimaya to the streets of Tulumai, here is a glimpse into Asmor's latest creations *and* a reimagined recipe from the infamous *Underworld Cookbook* itself.

Stowaway's Staple

Difficulty: ■■■□□ • **Prep Time:** 1 hour • **Inactive Time:** 3 hours • **Cook Time:** 30 minutes
Yield: 2 loaves • **Dietary Notes:** Vegetarian

While traveling through Benalia, Asmor met a grumpy thallid named Slimefoot. Asmor was surprised to learn that Slimefoot was born from stowaway spores on the Weatherlight, *a skyship that has saved Dominaria from destruction more than once. After sharing a meal in a meadow, Asmor invited Slimefoot to join her on her journey. He politely declined, preferring to feel the grass against his slow-moving feet as he wandered the world. As he strolled in the direction of Llanowar, he offered a tip for his signature bread: You can fill it with saprolings, but he'd prefer you use spinach.*

1 tablespoon canola oil

3 garlic cloves, minced

16 ounces spinach

1 ½ tablespoons active dry yeast

¾ cup milk, warmed (100°F)

4 cups bread flour

2 teaspoons kosher salt

¼ cup honey

3 eggs

2 egg yolks, egg whites reserved

¼ cup unsalted butter, room temperature

12 slices provolone cheese, cut in half

black sesame seeds

white sesame seeds

Heat a pan with canola oil over medium heat. Add the garlic and cook until softened, about 1 minute. Add the spinach and cook until wilted, about 3 minutes. Remove from the heat and set aside to cool.

Combine the yeast and milk. Allow the yeast to bloom, about 5 minutes. Combine the bread flour and salt in a large bowl. Add the milk, honey, 3 whole eggs, and 2 egg yolks. Continue to mix until it just comes together. While the dough begins to knead, add the butter 1 tablespoon at a time.

Knead the dough for 10 minutes. If the dough is too sticky, add additional flour. Shape into a ball and transfer to an oiled bowl. Cover and place in a warm area. Allow to proof for 2 hours, or until doubled in size.

Transfer the dough to a floured countertop and punch down. Divide into 6 equal portions and cover with a kitchen towel. Take one of the portions and roll it out into an 18-inch-wide rectangle. If the dough resists, allow it to rest for another 10 minutes.

Place 4 provolone halves across the dough. Top with a sixth of the spinach. Roll the dough over the filling and pinch to close. Gently roll the pinched section to smooth out the log.

Repeat this with the other 5 portions.

Continued on next page

To braid the dough, lay 3 portions vertically from you. Pinch the ends farthest away from you together and tuck the merged end under itself to keep it together. Take the left portion, lift it over the center portion, and lay it in between the two other portions. Take the right portion, lift it over the center portion, and lay it between the two other portions. Continue to repeat this pattern, switching between left and right until the bread is fully braided.

Once you reach the end of the dough, pinch it together and tuck it under the loaf. Transfer the braided bread onto a baking sheet with parchment paper. Cover with a kitchen towel and let rise for 1 hour, or until doubled in size. Repeat with the remaining dough.

Preheat oven to 375°F. Uncover the bread and brush with the reserved egg whites. Sprinkle white and black sesame seeds over the bread. Bake for 25 to 30 minutes, or until golden brown with an internal temperature of 190°F.

Necromancer's Pasta

Difficulty: ■■□□□ • **Prep Time:** 30 minutes • **Cook Time:** 30 minutes

Yield: 4 portions • **Dietary Notes:** Vegetarian

After parting ways with the thallid, Asmor headed to the Caligo Forest. There, the House of Vess had fallen into disrepair over the ages. Long ago, a young, idealistic healer by the name of Liliana once walked these halls. Every demon knows about Liliana, and during her time in the Underworld, Asmor had heard the tales about her demonic pacts and tribulations many times. To the demons, Liliana's story shows how anyone can be corrupted. But to Asmor, it was a story of redemption: If you are lost, you can find your way again. Just as cooking needed balanced flavors, something or someone could just as easily contain both light and shadow. Asmor thought long and hard about this duality as she noodled with noodles and cooking times, hoping to honor the necromancer who feared death in her own way.

16 ounces squid ink spaghetti

6 ounces spaghetti

kosher salt

ground black pepper

olive oil

2 shallots, thinly sliced

5 garlic cloves, minced

6 ounces chestnut mushrooms

5 ounces lion's mane mushrooms

3 ounces shiitake mushrooms, stems discarded

3 ounces oyster mushrooms

Note: *You can use any mushrooms you can get access to, but keep in mind the cook times on those mushrooms will be slightly different.*

1 ½ tablespoons dried thyme

1 cup white wine

2 tablespoons lemon zest

⅓ cup lemon juice

½ cup reserved pasta water

Heat enough water to cover the pasta in a large pot over high heat. When it reaches a boil, add 1 ½ tablespoons of salt. Cook the pasta until just al dente. Drain the pasta and reserve at least ½ cup of the water.

Heat a pan over medium-high heat with 1 tablespoon of olive oil. Add the shallots and cook until they become translucent. Add the garlic and let it cook for 5 minutes.

Add another tablespoon of olive oil to the pan and add the mushrooms. Cook until they have softened, about 5 to 8 minutes. Add the thyme and toss until coated. Taste the mushrooms and season with salt and pepper.

Add the white wine and cook until it reduces by half, about 2 minutes. Add the lemon zest and juice.

Add the cooked pasta. Slowly add the reserved pasta water until the sauce comes together with the pasta and everything is mixed well.

"ALL THE TIME IN THE WORLD" CROISSANTS

Difficulty: ■■■■ • **Prep Time:** 2 hours • **Inactive Time:** 50 hours • **Cook Time:** 20 - 25 minutes

Yield: 5 croissants • **Dietary Notes:** Vegetarian

Asmor cherished spending many happy hours in Niambi's kitchen during a restful visit to Femeref. Niambi, a healer of Zhalfirin descent, learned to cook from her mother, Subira, and her father, the planeswalker Teferi. Subira was a confident leader who preferred simple but daring recipes, while Teferi's baking was greatly influenced by his magic. He enjoyed time-consuming dishes that demanded his care and attention (and maybe a temporal wizardry, just in case).

Butter Block

12 tablespoons
   unsalted butter

Dough

⅔ cup + 1 tablespoon
   whole milk, warmed

1 tablespoon yeast

1 ¾ cups bread flour

3 tablespoons sugar

½ teaspoon cardamom

½ tablespoon kosher salt

1 teaspoon vanilla paste

1 ½ tablespoons unsalted
   butter, melted and cooled

Assembly

20 dark chocolate batons

1 large egg

2 tablespoons honey

Butter Block

Prepare a piece of parchment paper by drawing a 4-inch square on the backside of it. Cut the butter into equally thick pieces. Arrange the butter into the square on the parchment paper. Fold the parchment paper over the butter and make sure it is square-shaped. Take a rolling pin and smooth the butter into the square shape, merging the butter together into one solid piece. Wrap in plastic wrap and place in the refrigerator for at least 30 minutes to keep cold.

Note: *You can do this step ahead of time. The butter will stay good until its expiration date in this form. Day 1 of the dough preparation is a perfect time to do this.*

Day 1

Whisk together the yeast and milk in a cup and allow to bloom, about 3 minutes. Combine the bread flour, sugar, cardamom, and salt in a large bowl. Add the yeast mixture, vanilla paste, and melted butter.

Mix until it comes together. Transfer to a floured surface and knead until smooth. Place in a bowl, cover, and let rest for 10 minutes.

Take the rested dough and lightly pull the edge to the center and pat down. Repeat this around the entire dough. Flip over (smooth side facing up), cover, and rest for another 10 minutes. Once again, pull the edges to the center and pat down again. Flip, cover again, and rest for 25 minutes.

Transfer the dough to a sheet of parchment paper and roll out to a rough 7-inch square. Fold the parchment paper over the dough into a square. Use a rolling pin to make sure the dough fills the parchment square and is even. Wrap with plastic wrap and place in the refrigerator for 18 to 24 hours.

Continued on next page

Day 2

The next day, remove the dough from the plastic and parchment wrapping and place onto a floured surface. Lightly flour the top of the dough. With a rolling pin, roll each of the corners out.

Take the butter block out of its wrappings and place it in the center diagonally. Fold each of the dough corners over the butter, like sealing an envelope. Lightly tap with the rolling pin, cover with a kitchen towel, and let rest for 3 minutes.

Flip the dough over so the smooth side is facing upward. Lightly press down on the dough with the rolling pin. Roll out the dough to a 16-inch-long rectangle.

Note: *Try to roll the dough in one direction. If the dough ever seems like it is resisting, cover it with a kitchen towel and allow it to rest for 5 minutes before rolling again. This will help relax the gluten.*

Take the bottom of the rectangle and fold it ¾ of the way up. Take the top of the dough and fold it to have both edges touching one another. Take the new bottom of the rectangle and fold it to the new top. Turn it 90 degrees and lightly tap down with the rolling pin. Wrap in plastic wrap and let rest in the refrigerator for 90 minutes.

Remove the dough from the refrigerator, take it out of the plastic wrap, and place on a floured surface. Make sure the dough is positioned in the long direction, vertically from you. Take a rolling pin and tap down on the dough once more. Roll out the dough to a 16-inch-long rectangle.

Take the top of the rectangle and fold it two-thirds of the way down. Fold the bottom edge of the dough up and over. You should end up with a rough square shape at this point. Wrap with plastic wrap and place in the refrigerator for another 18 to 24 hours.

Note: *If you want to speed up this process, you can reduce the rest time to 2 hours and start the instructions for Day 3. Letting it rest overnight allows for the flavors to really mesh together.*

Day 3

Prepare a large baking tray with parchment paper. Remove the dough from the refrigerator, take it out of the plastic wrap, and place on a floured countertop. This time, roll the dough to a large rectangle (roughly 9 by 17 inches) that is ¼ inch thick.

Cut off any of the ends to make a smooth rectangle; the end result should roughly be an 8-by-15-inch rectangle. Cut into 5 equal rectangles (each at 8 by 5 inches, or as wide as the chocolate batons). Cover with a kitchen towel to avoid drying the dough out.

Take one of the dough rectangles and position it in the long direction, vertically from you. Place 2 chocolate batons at the bottom of the dough. Tightly roll the dough over the chocolate, toward the top, until the chocolate is just covered. Place 2 more chocolate batons on the dough and then continue to roll up until it is rolled up completely. Place, seam side down, on the prepared baking sheet. Repeat this with the remaining dough portions, making sure to give each of the croissants about 3 inches of space between each other. Cover with a kitchen towel and let rest in a warm spot for 1 to 2 hours, or until the croissants have doubled in size.

Preheat an oven to 400°F. Whisk the egg and honey together for an egg wash. Carefully brush each of the proofed croissants. Make sure to not apply any pressure that could cause the croissants to deflate. Place the baking sheet in the oven and reduce the heat to 340°F. Bake for 18 to 25 minutes, or until golden brown and cooked through.

Niambi's Spicy Bean Relish

Difficulty: ■■□□□ • **Prep Time:** 20 minutes • **Cook Time:** 30 minutes

Yield: 6 servings • **Dietary Notes:** Dairy-Free, Gluten-Free

To Asmor's delight, Niambi shared the first recipe she'd learned to cook as a child. Niambi and her mother had gone to their garden together, where Niambi picked the brightest peppers, tomatoes, and chilies. Then her father, Teferi, had laid out all the spices on the table and told her that a good recipe is like a good life: It takes insight, diligence, and care. Follow the rules, and it will turn out all right. Her mother disagreed. "Don't play it safe," Subira laughed and pointed to the chilies. "Make it extra spicy." Asmor heartily agreed with this advice.

1 teaspoon ground coriander

1 teaspoon ground cumin

1 teaspoon ground fenugreek

1 teaspoon cayenne pepper

½ teaspoon turmeric

½ teaspoon ground cardamom

½ teaspoon ground black pepper

1 tablespoon canola oil

1 onion, thinly sliced

½ teaspoon kosher salt

4 garlic cloves, minced

1 tablespoon ginger, minced

4 ounces tomato paste

1 red bell pepper, thinly sliced

1 yellow bell pepper, thinly sliced

1 red chili, chopped

5 Roma tomatoes, diced

3 carrots, julienned

One 15-ounce can baked beans

Combine the coriander, cumin, fenugreek, cayenne, turmeric, cardamom, and pepper in a small bowl. Set aside.

Heat a medium pot over medium-high heat. Add canola oil and let heat up for 1 minute. Add the onion and cook for 2 minutes. Add the salt and toss to coat. Cook until the onions have softened, 6 more minutes.

Add the garlic and ginger and cook for 2 minutes. Add the spices and mix in well. Add the tomato paste. Mix and cook for 2 minutes.

Add the bell peppers and red chili. Cook until the peppers have softened, about 5 minutes. Add the tomatoes and carrots and cook until the tomatoes have softened, about 5 minutes.

Add the baked beans and bring to a low simmer. Simmer for 5 minutes. Taste and season with additional salt and pepper.

Zhalfirin Grilled Flank Steak

Difficulty: ■■□□□ • **Prep Time:** 15 minutes • **Inactive Time:** 12 hours • **Cook Time:** 10 minutes

Yield: 2 - 3 servings • **Dietary Notes:** Dairy-Free, Gluten-Free

Zhalfir was her family's beloved homeland, but it was a land lost in time. As they cooked together, Niambi would tell Asmor the old stories, many of which involved great battles and celebratory feasts. As she and Asmor chopped peppers for the flank marinade, Niambi said that she believed that Zhalfir would return someday. When it did, Niambi knew that her people would stand together—shoulder to shoulder—as they did in the past. Asmor hoped the same.

4 garlic cloves, minced

2 tablespoons ginger, grated

2 teaspoons ground coriander

2 teaspoons paprika

1 teaspoon ground black pepper

½ teaspoon onion powder

½ teaspoon ground allspice

½ teaspoon cayenne pepper

½ teaspoon dried thyme

¼ cup olive oil

2 lbs flank steak

kosher salt

Whisk together the garlic, ginger, coriander, paprika, pepper, onion powder, allspice, cayenne pepper, thyme, and olive oil in a small bowl. Place the flank steak in a large airtight bag. Add the oil mixture and mix until the meat is completely covered. Seal and place in the refrigerator to marinate for at least 12 hours.

The next day, remove the steak from the bag and generously season with salt. Let rest at room temperature for 30 minutes.

Preheat a grill. Oil the grate to prevent the steak from sticking. Cook directly over the heat until it has a nice char on both sides and has reached an internal temperature of 110°F (43°C), about 5 to 10 minutes.

Transfer to a plate and cover in aluminum foil. Allow the meat to rest for 10 minutes before serving.

HEART OF YAVIMAYA

Difficulty: ■□□□□ • **Prep Time:** 20 minutes • **Inactive Time:** 30 minutes
Yield: 4 - 6 servings • **Dietary Notes:** Vegetarian, Gluten-Free

On a brief tour of Urborg, Asmor visited the remnants of the sentient forest of Yavimaya. Wishing for a glimpse of a kavu, Asmor headed deeper into the dense thicket. Soon, she found herself in a peaceful glade that seemed perfect for a short nap. But it was no natural sleep. As soon as her eyes closed, she heard a woman's voice speaking to her quietly. They talked of many things, but Multani's heart and the flowers that grow in Gaea's shadow stuck out in her mind most. When she awoke, she felt refreshed, hungry, and inspired to make a dish in honor of the Worldsoul. Asmor scribbled in her notebook a reminder to return to Urborg to further explore its culinary traditions—especially the fusion of Urborg and Phyrexian cuisine.

Dressing

⅓ cup olive oil

juice and zest of 2 lemons

2 tablespoons Dijon mustard

2 tablespoons honey

1 tablespoon dried oregano

1 teaspoon dried basil

1 teaspoon garlic powder

½ teaspoon onion powder

1 teaspoon kosher salt

Salad

28 ounces whole artichoke hearts,
　quartered

14 ounces hearts of palm,
　cut into bite-sized pieces

⅔ cup kalamata olives,
　pits removed and halved

1 cucumber, peeled and sliced

½ red onion, sliced

Whisk together all the ingredients for the dressing in a small bowl.

Place the artichoke hearts, hearts of palm, kalamata olives, cucumber, and red onion in a large bowl. Lightly toss to mix. Add the dressing and toss until combined. Allow to rest for at least 30 minutes in the refrigerator before serving.

HOMARIDS' BISQUE

Difficulty: ■■■□□ • **Prep Time:** 30 minutes • **Cook Time:** 1 hour • **Yield:** 4 servings • **Dietary Notes:** Shellfish

A new fishing village may stand on the site that was once Sekana, Madara, but the old ways and stories persist. While Asmor was visiting, the village elders spun tales of the tyrannical dragon who once ruled these lands, and it was in these legends that Asmor found her next inspiration. Even evil Elder Dragons must eat, and despite his megalomaniacal tendencies, Nicol Bolas had a discerning palate and a penchant for soup made from local seafood.

Lobster Stock

4 celery stalks, cut into large chunks

2 carrots, cut into large chunks

1 onion, quartered

1 head of garlic, cut in half

7 cups water

Three 4-ounce lobster tails

2 bay leaves

½ tablespoon black peppercorns

1 teaspoon cumin seeds

1 teaspoon caraway seeds

1 teaspoon fish sauce

Bisque

1 tablespoon unsalted butter

1 tablespoon olive oil

1 onion, diced

kosher salt

ground black pepper

2 celery stalks, diced

1 carrot, peeled and diced

3 garlic cloves

1 tablespoon tomato paste

3 tablespoons all-purpose flour

1 cup dry white wine

lobster stock

¼ cup heavy cream

Lobster Stock

Preheat oven to 400°F. Place the celery, carrots, onion, and garlic on a baking sheet. Roast the vegetables for 25 minutes.

Place a pot with water over medium-high heat and bring to a boil. Prepare the lobster tails by cutting them in half and removing the veins. Once the water comes to a boil, add the lobster tails and boil for 2 minutes, or until the shell has turned red. Transfer the lobster tails into a bowl with ice water. Do not discard the water in the pot that is boiling.

Remove the meat from the lobster tails. Store the lobster meat in an airtight container in the refrigerator for up to 2 days.

Place the lobster shells in the pot. Add the roasted vegetables, bay leaves, black peppercorns, cumin seeds, and caraway seeds. Bring the water back to a boil, reduce the heat, and simmer for 30 minutes.

After the stock has finished simmering, carefully strain the pot into another container to separate the stock from all the ingredients. Add the fish sauce to the stock. Can be stored in an airtight container in the refrigerator for up to 3 days.

Bisque

Place a large pot with butter and olive oil over medium-low heat. Add the onions and sauté until they become translucent, about 5 minutes. Season with salt and pepper. Add the celery and carrots. Cook for about 7 minutes, until the carrots have softened slightly.

Add the garlic and tomato paste and cook for another 2 minutes. Add the flour and heat until the flour is cooked, about 2 minutes. Add the wine and whisk until combined. Allow to simmer until it reduces by half.

Add the lobster stock and allow to simmer for 20 minutes. Remove from the heat and transfer the soup into a blender. Blend until smooth.

Return the soup to a pot and place over medium heat. Add the heavy cream and stir in. Taste and season with salt and pepper. Add the lobster meat and heat up, about 2 minutes.

Ooze-Infused Biscuits

Difficulty: ■■☐☐☐ • **Prep Time:** 30 minutes • **Inactive Time:** 45 minutes • **Cook Time:** 20 minutes
Yield: 16 biscuits • **Dietary Notes:** Vegetarian

According to the legends, Bolas insisted on the perfect oozy biscuits to enjoy with his Homarids' Bisque. The court appointed a homarid hunter and an ooze collector to keep up with Bolas's voracious demands. The resulting dishes are still remembered as his favorites despite the ages that have passed.

4 cups all-purpose flour

1 ½ teaspoons garlic powder

2 teaspoons sugar

1 tablespoon kosher salt

1 ½ tablespoons baking powder

1 ⅓ cups unsalted butter,
    cubed and chilled in the freezer
    for at least 20 minutes

1 ½ tablespoons chives, sliced

6 ounces cheddar cheese

1 ⅔ cups buttermilk, chilled

2 tablespoons unsalted butter, melted

Combine flour, garlic powder, sugar, salt, and baking powder in a large bowl. Add the cold butter and combine with your hands until it resembles coarse cornmeal. Place in the refrigerator and let rest for 15 minutes.

Remove from the refrigerator, add the chives and cheddar cheese, and toss until well dispersed. Add the buttermilk and stir until the dough barely comes together. Transfer to a floured work surface and knead until it just comes together.

Roll the dough into a 1-inch-tall rectangle. Fold the top third of the dough toward you. Next, fold the bottom third over the first fold. Reroll the dough again and repeat the fold. Reroll the dough once more to a 1-inch-tall rectangle.

Cut the dough into 16 portions. Place the biscuits on a baking sheet with parchment paper. Place in the freezer for 30 minutes.

Preheat oven to 425°F. Remove and brush each of the biscuits with melted butter. Bake for 15 to 20 minutes, or until golden brown. Transfer to a wire rack and allow to cool.

QUICKSILVER

Difficulty: ■□□□□ • **Prep Time:** 20 minutes • **Yield:** 1 drink • **Dietary Notes:** Vegan, Gluten-Free

As Asmor traveled onward, she heard the name Karn on more than one occasion. Her curiosity piqued, she followed tales of Karn from Tolaria through the Sardian Mountains to the Kher Ridges. By the time she reached the fateful Caves of Koilos, she had heard so many legends about his legacy that it was hard to determine truth from fiction. But be it history or story, she found the whole thing fascinating. She concocted the Quicksilver as a tribute to the memorable and profound silver golem himself. She hoped to herself (and to a footnote in her journal) that maybe one day, they could drink it together. But hold the powerstones, please.

2 ounces nigori sake

1 ounce cherry liqueur

2 ounces yuzu juice

½ teaspoon edible silver glitter

2 ounces club soda

ice

Place 3 ice cubes in a cocktail shaker. Add the nigori sake, cherry liqueur, yuzu juice, and silver glitter. Shake for 30 seconds. Prepare a tall glass with another 3 ice cubes. Strain the mixture into the prepared glass, discarding the ice in the cocktail shaker.

Top with the club soda, stir slightly, and serve.

BLACK LOTUS TEA

Difficulty: ■□□□□ • **Prep Time:** 5 minutes • **Cook Time:** 5 minutes
Yield: 2 cups • **Dietary Notes:** Vegetarian, Gluten-Free

Asmor knew that the Black Lotus would be hard to find and even more difficult to obtain. Her resourcefulness granted her a way to the secret vale where the precious flowers bloomed. These flowers contained surprising power, and Asmor considered carefully what to do with such a bounty. She could use them to be a conqueror, an emperor, a breaker of armies! But what does a chef need with those sorts of things? Amused, she instead brewed a perfect pot of Black Lotus Tea. While she sipped, she reflected on her adventures so far. She'd encountered a wandering thallid, heard the tales of the Elder Dragon, and walked in the footsteps of a gentle golem. There was still so much of Dominaria to be seen. She couldn't wait to see what she encountered next.

2 blue lotus flowers

1 tablespoon Assam black tea

2 teaspoons chamomile

2 tablespoons honey

2 cups hot water (200°F)

Place the lotus flowers, Assam black tea, chamomile, and honey in a small teapot. Add the hot water and steep for 5 minutes. Strain and serve.

GRANITE GARGOYLE WINGS

Difficulty: ■■■□□ • **Prep Time:** 30 minutes • **Inactive Time:** 15 - 36 hours • **Cook Time:** 40 minutes
Yield: 2 - 4 servings • **Dietary Notes:** Dairy-Free

So as not to disappoint the fans of her first book, the Underworld Cookbook, *Asmor has updated an old fan favorite! If gargoyles are uncommon in your corner of the Multiverse, a free-range or mesa chicken will do nicely.*

1 cup soy sauce

½ cup honey

¼ cup hot sauce

3 tablespoons gochujang

1 teaspoon sesame oil

2 teaspoons ginger powder

1 teaspoon garlic powder

½ teaspoon cayenne pepper

2 drops black food gel

2 lbs whole chicken wings

Combine everything but the chicken wings in a medium bowl. Whisk together until well combined. Add the chicken wings and make sure they are covered. Place in the refrigerator and marinate for 12 hours, up to 24 hours.

Place about 2 inches of water in a pot with a steamer basket and bring to a boil. Place the wings in the steamer basket.

Note: *Make sure to not overcrowd the basket or the wings will not steam correctly. It is best to do this in batches.*

Once the water is boiling, place the steamer basket in the pot and cover. Steam for 10 minutes. Remove the wings and pat them dry. Prepare a baking sheet lined with paper towels and a cooling rack on top. Place the wings on the rack and refrigerate the steamed wings for at least 3 hours, up to 8 hours.

Preheat your oven to 400°F. Replace the paper towel on the baking sheet with parchment paper. Bake the wings for 10 minutes. Flip and bake for another 15 to 20 minutes, or until the wings are cooked through.

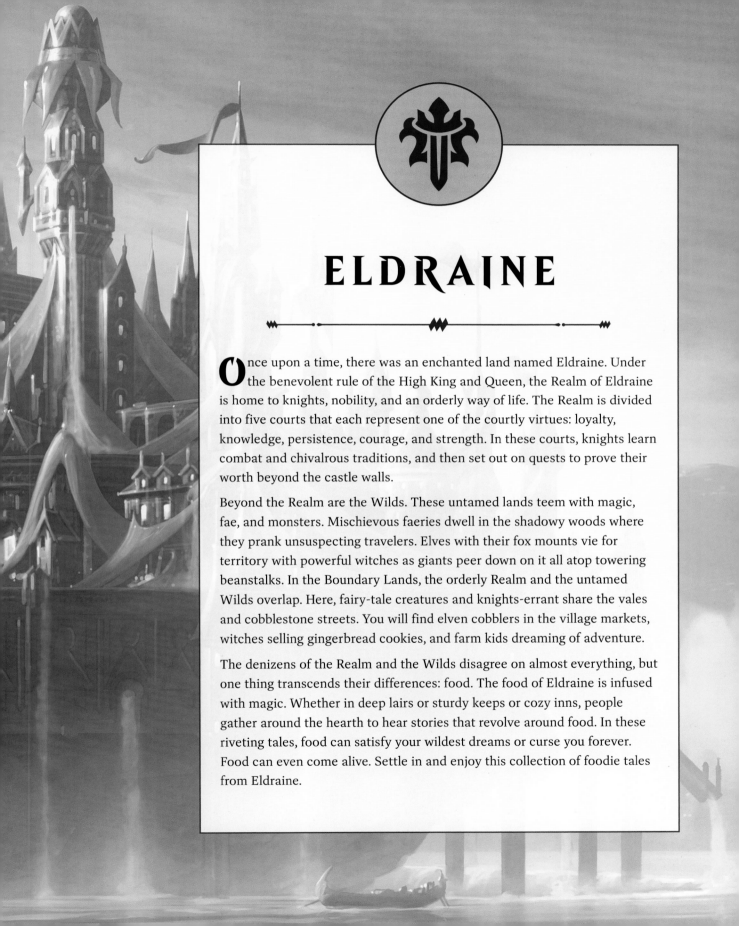

ELDRAINE

O nce upon a time, there was an enchanted land named Eldraine. Under the benevolent rule of the High King and Queen, the Realm of Eldraine is home to knights, nobility, and an orderly way of life. The Realm is divided into five courts that each represent one of the courtly virtues: loyalty, knowledge, persistence, courage, and strength. In these courts, knights learn combat and chivalrous traditions, and then set out on quests to prove their worth beyond the castle walls.

Beyond the Realm are the Wilds. These untamed lands teem with magic, fae, and monsters. Mischievous faeries dwell in the shadowy woods where they prank unsuspecting travelers. Elves with their fox mounts vie for territory with powerful witches as giants peer down on it all atop towering beanstalks. In the Boundary Lands, the orderly Realm and the untamed Wilds overlap. Here, fairy-tale creatures and knights-errant share the vales and cobblestone streets. You will find elven cobblers in the village markets, witches selling gingerbread cookies, and farm kids dreaming of adventure.

The denizens of the Realm and the Wilds disagree on almost everything, but one thing transcends their differences: food. The food of Eldraine is infused with magic. Whether in deep lairs or sturdy keeps or cozy inns, people gather around the hearth to hear stories that revolve around food. In these riveting tales, food can satisfy your wildest dreams or curse you forever. Food can even come alive. Settle in and enjoy this collection of foodie tales from Eldraine.

Rowan's Picnic Treats

One ordinary morning, Little Red Riding Rowan was enjoying a walk in the forest. A devious wolf stepped onto the path and tried to sweetly talk her into handing over the basket of goodies. Red Riding Rowan didn't appreciate his tone of voice. He might have big teeth, but she could smite him with sparks. They decided a picnic for two would be more fun than fighting, so they agreed to share the treats and soothe their hungry tempers. The wolf, of course, had planned to eat her afterward. But Rowan's Picnic Treats were so delightful, he decided to wait for another day.

Cinnamon Pinwheel Cookies

Difficulty: ■■■□□ • **Prep Time:** 1 hour • **Inactive Time:** 3 ½ hours • **Cook Time:** 15 minutes
Yield: 60 cookies • **Dietary Notes:** Vegetarian

Dough

3 ½ cups all-purpose flour

1 teaspoon baking soda

1 teaspoon baking powder

1 teaspoon kosher salt

1 cup sugar

½ cup unsalted butter,
    room temperature

2 eggs

1 teaspoon vanilla paste

1 teaspoon amaretto

4 ounces cream cheese

3 tablespoons heavy cream

Filling

¾ cup brown sugar

1 ½ tablespoons ground cinnamon

½ teaspoon grated nutmeg

½ teaspoon ground cardamom

3 tablespoons unsalted butter,
    melted and cooled

Combine flour, baking soda, baking powder, and salt in a medium bowl. Cream the butter in a large bowl. Mix in the sugar until combined and slightly fluffy.

Mix in the eggs one at a time. After the eggs are combined, add vanilla paste, amaretto, and cream cheese. Add half of the flour mixture. Mix in the heavy cream and then add the remainder of the flour mixture.

After the dough has been mixed well, split into three portions. Wrap each portion in plastic wrap and let it rest in the refrigerator for at least 3 hours.

Prepare the filling by combining brown sugar, cinnamon, nutmeg, and cardamom in a small bowl.

Take one of the dough portions out of the refrigerator. Roll out the dough into a rough rectangle (about 10 by 7 inches). Brush the melted butter onto the dough. Sprinkle a third of the cinnamon mixture onto the buttered dough. Carefully roll the dough tightly.

Pinch the ends of the rolled dough together to help avoid unrolling while baking. Wrap again in plastic wrap and place in the freezer for 30 minutes. Repeat with the remaining dough portions.

Preheat oven to 350°F. Take one of the portions out of the freezer. Cut the cookies into ½-inch-thick pieces. You should get about 20 cookies per set.

Arrange the cookies on a baking sheet with the spiral facing up. Bake for 10 to 13 minutes, or until the bottoms of the cookies have browned slightly. Repeat until all the dough has been cooked.

Continued on next page

BLUEBERRY SCONES

Difficulty: ■□□□ • **Prep Time:** 30 minutes • **Inactive Time:** 30 minutes • **Cook Time:** 40 minutes

Yield: 9 scones • **Dietary Notes:** Vegetarian

2 ¼ cups all-purpose flour

2 teaspoons baking powder

1 teaspoon kosher salt

½ teaspoon ground cinnamon

½ teaspoon grated nutmeg

⅓ cup sugar

zest of 3 small lemons

½ cup unsalted butter, cubed and frozen

1 cup frozen blueberries

1 cup buttermilk

1 teaspoon vanilla extract

1 teaspoon lemon juice

1 tablespoon heavy cream

Combine the flour, baking powder, salt, cinnamon, nutmeg, sugar, and lemon zest in a large bowl.

Add the cold butter and combine with your hands until it resembles coarse cornmeal. Mix in the blueberries. Combine the buttermilk, vanilla extract, and lemon juice in a small bowl. Add to the large bowl with the flour and mix until it just comes together, but do not overwork.

Transfer the dough onto the countertop and form into an 8-inch-wide square. Cut into 9 portions. Prepare a baking sheet with parchment paper and nonstick spray. Place the scones on the baking sheet. Place in the freezer and let rest for 30 minutes.

Preheat oven to 375°F. Brush the tops of the scones with heavy cream. Bake for 30 to 35 minutes, or until golden brown.

THUMBPRINT COOKIES

Difficulty: ■■□□□ • **Prep Time:** 1 hour • **Inactive Time:** 16 hours • **Cook Time:** 45 minutes
Yield: 24 - 30 cookies • **Dietary Notes:** Vegetarian

Cherry Jam

12 ounces fresh cherries, pitted

⅓ cup sugar

¼ teaspoon cinnamon

pinch of kosher salt

1 teaspoon lemon juice

Cookie

2 ⅓ cups all-purpose flour

½ teaspoon kosher salt

1 cup unsalted butter,
    room temperature

½ cup sugar

¼ cup brown sugar

1 teaspoon vanilla extract

1 egg

cherry jam

Cherry Jam

Place the cherries in a food processor and blend until smooth. Transfer to a saucepan and add the remaining ingredients. Place over medium-high and bring to a boil. Reduce the heat and simmer for 15 to 20 minutes, until the jam thickens.

Remove from the heat and transfer into an airtight container. Once cooled, cover and refrigerate for at least 12 hours and up to 2 weeks.

Cookie

Prepare a baking sheet with parchment paper and set aside. Combine flour and salt in a small bowl.

Cream the butter in a large bowl. Mix in the sugars until combined and slightly fluffy. Add the vanilla extract and egg. Mix until combined. Add the flour and mix until it just comes together.

Take about 1 to 2 tablespoons' worth of dough and roll into a ball. Place on the prepared baking sheet and lightly press down in the center with your thumb (or a teaspoon) to create an indentation. Repeat until all the dough is used. Place in the refrigerator and allow to chill for at least 2 hours.

Preheat oven to 375°F. Add the cherry jam into the center of the cookies, making sure it is filled slightly below the top. Place in the oven and bake for 12 to 15 minutes, or until the cookies are golden brown.

"Turn into a Pumpkin" Rolls

Difficulty: ■■■□□ • **Prep Time:** 1 hour • **Inactive Time:** 1 ½ hours • **Cook Time:** 20 minutes
Yield: 8 rolls • **Dietary Notes:** Vegetarian

Across the cobbles and over the dales, it is well known that King Algenus Kenrith and Queen Linden hold the finest celebrations in the Realm. Everyone is invited to enjoy jousting tournaments, name-guessing contests, and dancing in the grand hall. But there are unspoken rules that everyone must follow: No spinning wheels; always be polite to the frog; and everyone must leave before the clock strikes twelve. Anyone caught on the road after midnight risks an unfortunate transformation by the faeries! Veteran party-goers swear that it's better to enjoy these treats in the safety of your home than become a pumpkin yourself.

Dough

1 tablespoon active dry yeast

¾ cup milk, heated to 100°F

4 cups all-purpose flour

1 teaspoon kosher salt

1 teaspoon ground cinnamon

½ teaspoon ground ginger

¼ teaspoon ground allspice

⅛ teaspoon ground clove

¼ cup light brown sugar

¾ cup pumpkin puree

1 whole egg

1 egg yolk

4 tablespoons unsalted butter, room temperature

8 almonds

butcher twine

Egg Wash

1 egg

1 tablespoon honey

1 tablespoon milk

Brown Sugar Butter

½ cup unsalted butter, room temperature

⅓ cup dark brown sugar

½ teaspoon kosher salt

Combine the yeast and milk and let it rest for 5 minutes, allowing the yeast to bloom. Combine the all-purpose flour, salt, cinnamon, ginger, allspice, clove, and brown sugar in the large bowl of a stand mixer set with the dough hook attachment. Add the yeasted milk, pumpkin puree, egg, and egg yolk to the bowl and mix until the dough just comes together.

While kneading the dough, add the butter 1 tablespoon at a time. Knead the dough for 5 minutes. If the dough is too sticky, add 1 tablespoon of flour at a time. If it is too dry, add 1 tablespoon of milk at a time.

Transfer to an oiled bowl, cover, and let rest for 1 hour or until doubled in size. Once doubled, punch down and knead. Prepare a baking sheet with parchment paper.

Cut eight 2 ½-foot-long pieces of butcher twine and set aside. Divide the dough into 8 equal portions. Shape into round balls and place on the baking sheet. Cover with a kitchen towel.

Take one of the portions and a piece of butcher twine. Spray the butcher twine with nonstick spray. Place the dough in the center of the twine. Lightly tie the twine around the dough into 8 sections. Tie the string together at the bottom and cut off excess string. Place the dough back on the parchment paper, knot side down. Repeat with the remaining portions.

Note: *This is done to give the rolls the shape of a pumpkin. This step can be skipped if you would like round rolls.*

Once all the dough has been shaped, let rest for 30 minutes, or until doubled in size. In a small bowl, whisk the egg, honey, and milk for the egg wash. Remove the kitchen towel from atop the dough and brush each of the buns with the egg wash.

Preheat oven to 375°F. Bake for 16 to 19 minutes, or until golden and cooked through. Remove and allow to cool for 20 minutes before carefully removing the string. To add a stem to your pumpkin rolls, you can place an almond in the center.

Before serving the rolls, combine all the ingredients for the brown sugar butter and mix until well incorporated. This can be stored in an airtight container in the refrigerator, but it is best served at room temperature right after it is mixed together. Serve with the pumpkin rolls.

Garruk's Skewer

Difficulty: ■■□□□ • **Prep Time:** 45 minutes • **Inactive Time:** 12 hours • **Cook Time:** 20 minutes
Yield: 5 skewers • **Dietary Notes:** Dairy-Free

Over mountains and between valleys, there lived a huntsman named Garruk Wildspeaker who had been cursed by a witch. He didn't want to hurt anyone, so he went deep into the forest to live a simple life as a hunter, taking only what he needed to survive. One night, he found two lost children wandering in the forest. He took them back to his campfire and fed them the last of the food he had. Well-fed and warm, the children revealed that they were the prince and princess of Eldraine. To thank him for saving them, they promised when they met again, they would remove his curse forever. And so it came to be.

2 tablespoons soy sauce

1 tablespoon honey

2 tablespoons hoisin

½ teaspoon ground cinnamon

½ teaspoon ground fennel

½ teaspoon ground Sichuan peppercorns

¼ teaspoon ground star anise

¼ teaspoon ground clove

Note: *If you have a Chinese five spice blend, you can replace these spices listed above with 2 teaspoons of Chinese five spice.*

4 garlic cloves, minced

One 1-inch piece of ginger, grated

1 lb pork tenderloin, cut into cubes

½ red onion, cut into bite-sized pieces

½ cup fresh pineapple, cut into bite-sized pieces

Combine soy sauce, honey, hoisin, cinnamon, fennel, Sichuan peppercorns, star anise, clove, garlic, and ginger in an airtight container. Add the pork tenderloin and toss to coat. Seal and place in the refrigerator overnight.

The next day, place 5 wooden skewers to soak in water for 30 minutes prior to grilling. Remove the pork from the marinade. Place a piece of meat on the skewer followed by two pieces of red onion and a slice of pineapple. Repeat until you have 5 pieces of meat on the stick. Repeat this step until all the pork is used.

Cook the skewers for 7 to 10 minutes on a preheated grill. Flip to crisp all sides and cook the pork through.

GINGERBRUTE

Difficulty: ■■■☐☐ • **Prep Time:** 45 minutes • **Inactive Time:** 2 hours • **Cook Time:** 15 - 18 minutes
Yield: 24 - 30 large cookies • **Dietary Notes:** Vegetarian

Would you believe, dear reader, that a gingerbread cookie named Syr Ginger came to life in a castle kitchen? She expected to become a scullery maid tormented by her evil step-cookies. Instead, she met her true love, a crispy rogue with black-button eyes and a charming grin. Bursting with happiness, the two made plans to run away together. But a cursed huntsman attacked the castle and callously devoured her beau. With the terrible sounds of crunching in her ears, Syr Ginger transformed into the relentless cookie monster known as Gingerbrute. Some say she wanders the land to this day, seeking vengeance on the man who crumbled her heart.

Gingerbread Cookie

4 ½ cups all-purpose flour

1 ½ tablespoons ground ginger

1 ½ tablespoons ground cinnamon

½ teaspoon cayenne pepper

1 teaspoon ground allspice

½ teaspoon nutmeg, grated

¼ teaspoon ground cloves

1 teaspoon baking powder

1 teaspoon kosher salt

1 cup unsalted butter,
   room temperature

½ cup brown sugar

¼ cup sugar

¼ cup honey

1 tablespoon fresh ginger, grated

½ cup unsulfured molasses

2 teaspoons vanilla extract

1 egg

Gingerbread Cookie

Combine the flour, ginger, cinnamon, cayenne, allspice, nutmeg, cloves, baking powder, and salt in a medium bowl. Cream the butter in a large bowl. Add the sugars and mix until combined and slightly fluffy. Add the honey, fresh ginger, molasses, vanilla extract, and egg. Finally, add the flour mixture and mix until it is just combined. Split the dough in half.

Take one of the halves and transfer onto a sheet of parchment paper. Lightly flour the portion and then cover with another sheet of parchment paper. Roll the dough out to ¼- to ½-inch thickness. Cover with another sheet of parchment paper and place in the refrigerator to rest for at least 1 hour. Repeat this step with the other half of the dough.

Preheat oven to 350°F. After the dough has rested, take one of the dough portions and place it on a very floured surface. Carefully use a cookie cutter to cut out the cookies. Place the cutout cookies on a baking sheet covered in parchment paper. Reshape the remaining dough and roll it out once again. Cut out more cookies. Repeat this until you have used up all the dough. Bake for 15 to 18 minutes.

Note: *You can use any cookie cutter you would like. If you want to make these look like the Gingerbrute, draw out the character on a piece of paper and cut that. Place the cutout on the dough and, with a sharp knife, cut out the Gingerbrute. Be careful when transferring these cutouts to the baking sheet because some sections might be a bit more fragile.*

Allow the cookies to completely cool before icing them.

Continued on next page

Royal Icing

½ cup confectioners' sugar

1 teaspoon meringue powder

1 to 2 tablespoons water

Assembly

Mini chocolate chips

Royal Icing

Combine the confectioners' sugar and meringue powder in a medium bowl. Add 1 tablespoon of water. With a hand mixer, whisk together while slowly adding additional water as needed.

Note: *The end result should be loose, but not too loose. When the icing drizzles off the hand mixer, it should make a smooth surface in about 10 seconds. Be careful to not add too much water, but if you do, just add additional confectioners' sugar.*

Assembly

Once the icing has reached the correct consistency, transfer to a piping bag. Decorate your cookies to your liking, such as with fun faces and unique clothing. To add the mini chocolate chips, place a small amount of royal icing on the cookie and then press the chocolate chip on the cookie. Let rest for at least 1 hour before serving to allow the icing to harden.

OKO'S ELK

Difficulty: ■■■□□ • **Prep Time:** 1 hour • **Cook Time:** 4 hours
Yield: 6 servings • **Dietary Notes:** Dairy-Free

Edgewall Village had a serious elk problem, thanks to the trickster Oko. At his behest, the marauding elk took over the cobblestones, rampaged through the mead hall, and tossed the mayor onto the roof of town hall! Oko kindly offered to rid the village of the elk, and he only wanted a small fortune in return. Desperate, the Edgewall elders agreed, and Oko merrily led the herd into the forest. Oko tried to send the elk back to the village for more shenanigans. Unfortunately, the elk took a shine to Oko and refused to leave the side of their new master. According to legends, they are following him to this day.

3 lbs elk stew meat, cut into large pieces

kosher salt

ground black pepper

canola oil

3 tablespoons all-purpose flour

1 onion, sliced

1 red onion, sliced

3 carrots, peeled and cut into
    1-inch-thick medallions

7 garlic cloves, thinly sliced

3 cups red wine

1 tablespoon dried thyme

1 tablespoon sage

2 teaspoons juniper berries, crushed

3 tablespoons tomato paste

1 cup beef broth

2 bay leaves

12 ounces pearl onions

¼ cup + 2 tablespoons water

8 ounces mushrooms, quartered

1 tablespoon cornstarch

egg noodles

Preheat oven to 325°F. Generously season the elk with salt and pepper.

Heat a dutch oven over medium heat and add 1 tablespoon of canola oil. Add a single layer of the elk, being careful not to overcrowd the pan. Brown all sides of the meat. Remove and place on a plate. Add additional canola oil, if needed, and continue this process until all the elk has been browned. Toss the elk in all-purpose flour and set aside.

Add another tablespoon of canola oil to the dutch oven. Add the white and red onions and carrots. Cook until the onion is softened, about 5 minutes.

Add the garlic and cook for another 2 minutes. Add the elk back to the dutch oven and stir together. Mix in the red wine, thyme, sage, juniper berries, tomato paste, and beef broth. Stir together until the tomato paste has incorporated with the rest of the liquid.

Add the bay leaves and cover with a lid. Place in the oven and cook for 3 hours, or until the elk is tender.

About 45 minutes before the elk is done, bring 3 cups of water to a boil. Place the pearl onions in a bowl and pour the hot water over them. Allow them to sit in the bowl for 30 seconds.

Carefully transfer the pearl onions into a bowl with ice-cold water. Cut the butt ends off the onions and then remove the peels.

Place a pan over medium-high heat. Spray with nonstick spray and cook the pearl onions until they start to brown. Add ¼ cup of water and cover. Reduce the heat to medium and allow the onions to soften (do not allow them to become mushy and lose their shape), about 15 minutes. Remove any remaining liquid and set aside until the stew is ready.

Continued on next page

In another pan, over medium-high heat, cook the mushrooms until just browned. Set aside until the stew is ready.

Once the stew has finished cooking, carefully pour the contents of the dutch oven through a mesh strainer with a bowl underneath to collect the liquid.

Place the liquid in a saucepan and heat over medium heat. In a small bowl, combine the cornstarch and 2 tablespoons of cold water. Once the sauce is slightly simmering, whisk in the cornstarch slurry and mix until the sauce has slightly thickened.

Return the elk and veggies back to the dutch oven. Pour in the thickened sauce and add the pearl onions and mushrooms. Stir the contents together. Serve over a bowl of egg noodles.

POISONED APPLE CIDER

Difficulty: ■□□□□ • **Prep Time:** 5 minutes

Yield: 1 cup • **Dietary Notes:** Vegetarian, Gluten-Free

Child, be wary as you journey through the deep, dark wood. A kindly traveler might be a witch hiding behind a hood. For a small price, she offers you a green-apple drink. But her plans for you are not what you think. One sip might give you death's lasting relief. Or it might give you power beyond belief. Be wary!

3 ice cubes

2 ounces Midori

1 ounce Japanese whisky

½ ounce yuzu juice

4 ounces sparkling apple cider

Place 3 ice cubes in a cocktail shaker. Add the Midori, Japanese whisky, and yuzu juice. Shake for 30 seconds. Strain the mixture into a tall glass, leaving the ice in the cocktail shaker.

Top with the sparkling apple cider, stir, and serve.

HAPPILY EVER AFTER

Difficulty: ■☐☐☐☐ • **Prep Time:** 5 minutes • **Cook Time:** 15 minutes

Yield: 1 cup • **Dietary Notes:** Vegetarian, Gluten-Free

Good prince and princesses, the night has come. It's time to sleep. Our tales are done.

2 tablespoons dried chamomile

1 tablespoon dried lavender

1 teaspoon valerian root

1 lemon peel

1 tablespoon honey

½ cup water (200°F)

1 cup milk

Place the chamomile, lavender, valerian root, lemon peel, and honey in a small teapot. Add the hot water and steep for 5 minutes. Strain and serve in a mug.

Heat the milk in a saucepan over medium-high heat. Bring to a simmer. Add to the mug with the tea, stir, and serve.

INNISTRAD

Tibalt tore off a chunk of crusty bread and mused about his homeland while he chewed. Innistrad was a gothic playground with a well-defined pecking order: Monsters run the joint and humans rightfully cower in their cottages wearing unfashionable hats and praying for deliverance. The vampires are at the top of the social order, just below the devils, of course. The fanged menace Sorin Markov fancies himself to be *the* Lord of Innistrad because he "saved" the humans. Tibalt wrinkled his nose and took another annoyed bite. If anyone was the true celebrity of this plane, it was him: Tibalt. He was the rogue who knew all the gossip from Thraben to Stensia. Everyone always dwelled on the "pain" part of his magic, but they conveniently forgot about the "empathic" part. He was a sensitive devil, after all. He liked to dive deep into others' emotions, giving him insight into the juiciest scandals.

Tibalt believed that rumors are like candy to be savored. He knew where the missing archangel Avacyn was years before Liliana ruined the party. It was he who found the eldritch clues long before Jace stumbled into the Drownyard. He knew that the vampire lords Edgar and Olivia were going to get hitched before they did! And he's the only one who knows what Emrakul is doing inside the silver moon. Tibalt slumped, hurting his own feelings. Who would believe it? No one ever believes poor Tibalt.

TEA WITH TIBALT

Difficulty: ■□□□□ • **Prep Time:** 5 minutes • **Cook Time:** 6 minutes

Yield: 2 cups • **Dietary Notes:** Vegan, Gluten-Free

Join Tibalt as he shares some lore about the hottest names in Innistrad's history. Sorin might be the Scion of Smolder, but Tibalt would always be the Greatest of Gossipmongers, and he had plenty of tea to spill.

1 tablespoon pu-erh tea

1 teaspoon dried lemongrass

1 teaspoon dried burdock

2 teaspoons dried ginger

2 teaspoons dried orange peels

2 cups hot water (200°F)

Place the pu-erh tea, lemongrass, burdock, ginger, and orange peels in a small teapot. Add the hot water and steep for 6 minutes. Strain and serve.

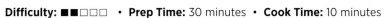

TIBALT'S DEVILED EGGS

Difficulty: ■■□□□ • **Prep Time:** 30 minutes • **Cook Time:** 10 minutes
Yield: 16 servings • **Dietary Notes:** Vegetarian, Gluten-Free

No tea party is complete without some delectable goodies, like Tibalt's special recipe for eggs. Sure, you can go to the chicken coop, which will provide for a wonderful dish. But Tibalt prefers to use the eggs of the moon-heron. The people of Innistrad see the moon-heron as a symbol of hope for their beloved Avacynian Church. Tibalt says: Who needs hope when you've got garlic and Dijon?

8 eggs

4 whole black garlic bulbs

¼ cup yogurt

1 tablespoon Dijon mustard

2 teaspoons lemon juice

½ teaspoon ground fennel

cayenne pepper

Place the eggs in a pot and fill with enough water to cover completely. Cover with a lid and place over medium-high heat. Bring to a boil for 7 minutes.

Once the timer for the eggs has finished, immediately take the pot off the stove and place under cold running water. Move the eggs to a bowl with ice cubes and cold water. Let sit for 3 minutes. Carefully de-shell the eggs and set aside.

Cut the eggs in half. Scoop out the egg yolks and place in a food processor with black garlic, yogurt, Dijon mustard, and lemon juice. Pulse until smooth. Add the fennel and mix to combine. Fill each of the egg whites with the egg yolk mixture. Garnish with cayenne pepper.

Black Heart Quiche

Difficulty: ■■■□□ • **Prep Time:** 45 minutes • **Cook Time:** 1 ½ hours
Yield: 12 small quiches • **Dietary Notes:** Vegetarian

For all of you who thought this was a recipe named for Tibalt…it's not! It's a culinary celebration of the black heart of Innistrad itself. So, raise your fork to those gothic betrayals, haunted castles, stormy nights, lurking monsters, demonic cults, and things that go bump in the night! Tibalt celebrates all your dark deliciousness.

Filling

2 tablespoons olive oil

2 large onions, sliced

½ lb baby portobello mushrooms, stems removed and sliced

½ lb shiitake mushrooms, stems removed and sliced

kosher salt

Egg Custard

4 eggs

½ cup heavy cream

½ cup whole milk

Quiche

1 ½ puff pastry sheets

6 ounces feta cheese

Heat a medium frying pan with 1 tablespoon olive oil over medium heat. Add the onions, toss, and coat with the oil. Cook the onions until they turn translucent, about 2 minutes.

Add a pinch of salt, stir, and reduce the heat to medium-low. Continue cooking and stirring occasionally until the onions become golden and caramelized, about 40 to 60 minutes. Remove from the heat, transfer the onions to a plate, and set aside to cool.

Place the same pan over medium heat. Add another tablespoon of olive oil. Add the mushrooms and cook until golden brown, about 10 minutes. Transfer to the plate with the onions and mix. Set aside until you are ready to assemble.

Whisk together the eggs, heavy cream, and whole milk until well combined.

Preheat oven to 400°F. Prepare a muffin tin by spraying with nonstick spray. Split the puff pastry sheets into 12 squares. Place each of the squares in one of the wells of the muffin tin. Press the center to the bottom of the well and lightly press the sides against the walls.

Split the feta cheese between the 12 portions. Top each with the onion-and-mushroom mixture. Carefully pour the egg mixture on top. Place in the oven and bake for 20 minutes, or until set. Transfer to a cooling rack and let cool for at least 10 minutes before cutting to serve.

GERALF'S FRANKEN-CHICKEN

Difficulty: ■■□□□ • **Prep Time:** 30 minutes • **Inactive Time:** 24 hours • **Cook Time:** 1 - 1 ½ hours
Yield: 1 whole chicken • **Dietary Notes:** Gluten-Free

Murderously competitive, Gisa and Geralf were necromancers who would do anything to best each other. The siblings vehemently disagree on the preparation of the undead, employing vastly different techniques to reanimate their targets. They have gone toe-to-toe repeatedly to prove who's better with a corpse, always ending in an even score. Their grudge grew to include a face-off in the kitchen over chicken. Geralf brought his mad stitching skills to the table and crafted full-bodied fare that befits his lofty ambitions.

Black Garlic Butter

¼ cup unsalted butter,
   room temperature

pinch of kosher salt

2 whole black garlic bulbs

Whole Chicken

5 lbs whole chicken

kosher salt

ground black pepper

1 head of garlic, cut in half

1 lemon, sliced

3 rosemary sprigs

3 thyme sprigs

Combine all the ingredients for the black garlic butter in a bowl. Mix until all ingredients just come together. Set aside.

Take the chicken and flip it so the back is facing up. Using a pair of kitchen shears, cut along both sides of the spine of the chicken and remove it.

Note: *You can use the spine in a chicken stock or broth.*

Flip the chicken and spread the legs so they are lying flat. Press firmly on the breastbone until it cracks. The chicken should now be lying quite flat.

Carefully separate the chicken skin from the chicken. Take the black garlic butter and rub it between the chicken and the skin, spreading it evenly over the breast and legs.

Prepare a baking sheet with a wire rack. Transfer the chicken onto the rack, keeping it flat. Generously season with salt and pepper. Put the chicken in the refrigerator, uncovered, for 18 to 24 hours.

Take the chicken out of the refrigerator. Use the paper towel to clean up any liquid or blood that might have ended up on the pan while it rested. Preheat an oven to 375°F.

Remove the chicken from the wire rack. Check again to clean up any blood that may have dropped onto the baking sheet. Place the wire rack without the chicken back on the baking sheet. Top the rack with the garlic, lemon, rosemary, and thyme. Place the chicken on top.

Bake for 1 to 1 ½ hours, or until the internal temperature reads 165°F. Remove from the oven and cover with aluminum foil. Let it rest for 10 minutes before cutting to serve.

GISA'S "RAISE 'EM RIGHT" CHICKEN

Difficulty: ■■□□□ • **Prep Time:** 30 minutes • **Inactive Time:** 24 hours • **Cook Time:** 1 ½ - 2 hours
Yield: 1 whole chicken • **Dietary Notes:** Dairy-Free

Geralf tried to impose some rules on the chicken wars, but his sister, Gisa, laughed at his attempts to make her use the proper cookware. She headed to the graveyard to raise the tastiest chicken horror. Her zombie army cheered wildly for her invigorating entry, but Geralf refused to concede the contest. Tibalt laughed wildly, imagining their faces when the competition again came to a draw.

Brine

3 cups water

¼ cup shiro miso

¼ cup soy sauce

¼ cup sugar

1 kombu, broken into chunks

4 dehydrated shiitake mushrooms

One 2-inch piece of ginger, sliced

Whole Chicken

4 lbs whole chicken

2 lemons, cut in half

Spice Rub

3 tablespoons bonito flakes, ground

1 nori sheet

1 dried shiitake mushroom

1 tablespoon garlic powder

1 tablespoon gochugaru

Combine water, shiro miso, soy sauce, and sugar in a large bowl. Place the chicken, kombu, shiitake mushrooms, and ginger in a large sealable bag. Add the brine and seal shut. Place the bag in a large bowl to avoid any messes if the bag breaks. Place in the refrigerator and let rest for 12 hours, up to 24 hours.

Preheat oven to 375°F. Remove the chicken from the brine, discarding all the brine ingredients. Pat the chicken dry and place on a wire rack on a baking sheet. Combine all the ingredients of the spice rub in a small bowl. Rub the chicken thoroughly, inside and out, with the spice rub.

Insert the lemon in the cavity of the chicken. Bake, breast side up, for 1 ½ to 2 hours or until the internal temperature reads 165°F. Remove from the oven and cover with aluminum foil. Let it rest for 10 minutes before carving.

Endless Shanks of the Dead

Difficulty: ■■■□□ • **Prep Time:** 1 hour • **Inactive Time:** 24 hours • **Cook Time:** 4 hours • **Yield:** 4 servings

Tibalt knew all the scuttlebutt about Thalia and her nemesis, Liliana. Years ago, Thalia was a promising young holy warrior cathar. Despite her conviction, the Dark Queen dogged her footsteps for years. Eventually, Liliana compelled Thalia to break the Helvault, which released all the trapped demons into the world. To add insult to injury, Liliana left a mess of zombies all over Thraben and expected Thalia to clean them up.

Lamb Shank

4 lamb shanks

olive oil

kosher salt

ground black pepper

2 carrots, roughly chopped

1 onion, roughly chopped

1 fennel bulb, roughly chopped

1 head of garlic, roughly chopped

3 tablespoons tomato paste

2 tablespoons all-purpose flour

2 cups dry red wine

4 cups beef broth

2 rosemary sprigs

3 thyme sprigs

2 bay leaves

Horseradish Gorgonzola Mashed Potatoes

2 ½ lbs russet potatoes, peeled and quartered

1 bay leaf

2 dried shiitake mushrooms

kosher salt

ground black pepper

¼ cup unsalted butter

1 cup cream cheese

½ cup gorgonzola

2 tablespoons grated horseradish

Lamb Shank

Prepare a baking sheet with a wire rack. Rub the lamb shanks with salt and pepper. Place in the refrigerator and let rest for 12 to 24 hours.

Preheat oven to 350°F. Heat a dutch oven over medium heat and add 1 tablespoon of olive oil. Add 2 of the lamb shanks and sear until browned, about 3 to 5 minutes per side. Once all sides are browned, transfer to a plate. Repeat this step with the remaining lamb shanks.

Add another tablespoon of olive oil to the dutch oven. Add the carrots, onion, fennel bulb, and garlic. Cook until the vegetables have softened, about 8 to 10 minutes. Add the tomato paste and flour. Toss together until well mixed and cook for another 2 minutes.

Add the red wine and deglaze the pan. Bring to a simmer and cook until it reduces by half, about 5 minutes. Add the broth and lamb shanks. Add the rosemary, thyme, and bay leaves. Cover and transfer to the oven. Allow to bake for 3 hours, until the shanks are tender.

Remove the shanks from the dutch oven and transfer to a plate. Wrap in aluminum foil and allow to rest.

Strain the broth and discard the vegetables and herbs. Place the broth in a saucepan and heat over medium-high heat. Bring to a simmer, reduce the heat to medium, and allow to simmer for 25 minutes, or until it reduces by two-thirds.

To serve, place a portion of mash potatoes on a plate. Top with a shank and a generous portion of the sauce.

Horseradish Gorgonzola Mashed Potatoes

Heat a pot with water, potatoes, bay leaf, dried shiitake mushrooms, and a pinch of salt over high heat. Bring to a boil and then reduce the heat and simmer for 15 to 20 minutes, or until the potatoes are tender.

Drain and remove the bay leaf and shiitake mushrooms.

Place the pot back on the stove and add the butter and cream cheese. Add the potatoes and mash until smooth.

Add the gorgonzola and horseradish and mix. Season with salt and pepper to taste.

THALIA'S OFFERING

Difficulty: ■■■□□ • **Prep Time:** 45 minutes • **Inactive Time:** 2 ½ hours • **Cook Time:** 20 minutes
Yield: 8 garlic knots • **Dietary Notes:** Vegetarian

As holy members of the Avacyn Church, Thalia and her friend Odric held fast to their order even during Avacyn's absence. But Commander Odric fell to vampirism, and Thalia blamed herself. Grieving her stalwart companion, Thalia turned to baking. Somebody—definitely not Tibalt—told Thalia that garlic kept vampires at bay, and she believed it. Ever since then, she's been baking these scrumptious garlic knots by the dozen. Tibalt felt a tad guilty, knowing that the garlic would not ward off a Voldaren or Markov anytime soon. But he couldn't reveal the truth and feel greater guilt by denying locals the delicious bread more beloved than the Blessed Sleep.

Dough

2 ¾ cups + 3 tablespoons bread flour

1 cup milk, heated to 100°F

1 tablespoon active dry yeast

1 tablespoon kosher salt

¼ cup granulated sugar

2 teaspoons garlic powder

1 egg

4 whole black garlic bulbs, mashed

4 tablespoons unsalted butter, room
   temperature

Topping

4 garlic cloves, minced

6 tablespoons unsalted butter, melted

2 teaspoons dried oregano

1 tablespoon black sesame seeds

1 tablespoon dried basil

pinch of kosher salt

Place 3 tablespoons bread flour and ⅓ cup milk in a saucepan. Heat over medium-high heat and whisk until it comes together into a thick paste, about 1 minute. Set aside and allow to cool.

Combine the yeast and the remaining milk and let it rest for 5 minutes, allowing the yeast to become active. Combine 2 ¾ cups bread flour, salt, and sugar in the large bowl of a stand mixer set with the whisk attachment. Add the flour paste, yeasted milk, and egg to the bowl and mix until it just comes together.

While the dough begins to knead, add the butter 1 tablespoon at a time. Add the black garlic in. Knead the dough for 5 minutes. If the dough is too sticky, add 1 tablespoon of flour at a time. If it is too dry, add 1 tablespoon of milk at a time.

Transfer to an oiled bowl, cover, and let rest for 1 hour, or until doubled in size. Once doubled, punch down and knead. Prepare a baking sheet by placing parchment paper down.

Divide the dough into 8 portions. Take one of the portions and roll it out into a long tube that you can tie. Carefully tie into a knot and tuck the ends under the bottom of the roll. Place on the baking sheet. Repeat with the remaining portions.

Cover the dough with a kitchen towel and let rest for 30 minutes, or until doubled in size.

Preheat oven to 400°F. Combine the ingredients for the topping in a small bowl. Brush each of the knots with the topping. Bake for 20 to 25 minutes, or until golden brown and cooked through.

TEFERI'S "SLOW THE SUNSET"

Difficulty: ■■■□ • **Prep Time:** 1 hour • **Cook Time:** 15 minutes • **Yield:** 4 rolls • **Dietary Notes:** Dairy-Free, Gluten-Free

Allegedly, the two planeswalkers, Teferi and Wrenn, bonded on a little stroll through the Kessig forest. Teferi was an ancient planeswalker who meddled in the affairs of well, everyone. Wrenn was a mysterious dryad who could merge with trees. The unexpected friendship forged in that autumnal forest would have important implications for the Multiverse. But before saving everyone, they had to solve a pressing problem: what to have for dinner? Teferi was having so much fun that he didn't want the day to end. So he conjured a succulent dish in honor of the colors of the setting sun.

4 eggs

2 teaspoons sugar

1 carrot, peeled and julienned

9 ounces spinach

3 cups cooked short-grain rice, still warm

1 teaspoon white sesame seeds, lightly crushed

2 teaspoons black sesame seeds, lightly crushed

1 tablespoon sesame oil

pinch of kosher salt

4 sheets of gim

1 cucumber, peeled and julienned

4 danmuji

Zhalfirin Grilled Flank Steak (page 51), cut into thin strips

tonkatsu sauce

Whisk the eggs and sugar. Heat a nonstick 10-inch pan over medium heat. Spray with nonstick spray. Once heated, add half of the egg mixture and swirl to cover the bottom of the pan. Cover the pan and let cook until the top has just set. Carefully remove the egg and transfer to a cutting board. Repeat with the remaining portion of eggs.

Cut the eggs into long strips, about ½ inch wide. Set aside.

Bring a pot of salted water to a boil. Place the carrots in the water and let cook for 2 minutes. Remove the carrots and place on a plate with a paper towel to drain.

Next, add the spinach to the pot and cook until wilted, about 2 minutes. Drain and run under cold water. Squeeze out the excess liquid from the spinach. Set aside.

Combine the cooked rice, sesame seeds, sesame oil, and salt in a bowl. Divide into 4 portions, and keep covered with a moist paper towel.

Place a sheet of gim on a sushi mat. Wet your hands and add a thin layer of rice onto the gim, leaving about 1 inch at the top empty.

Place the carrots, spinach, cucumber, danmuji, and steak in the center of the rice. Carefully and tightly roll the sushi together using the sushi mat. At this point, the rolls can be wrapped in plastic wrap and stored in the refrigerator for up to 3 days. Repeat this with the remaining ingredients.

Cut the rolls in half using a sharp knife. In between each cut, wipe the knife blade with a wet kitchen towel. Cut each of the halves into 3 to 4 pieces. Serve with tonkatsu sauce for dipping.

WRENN AND SIX SALAD

Difficulty: ■■□□□ • **Prep Time:** 30 minutes • **Cook Time:** 10 minutes
Yield: 4 servings • **Dietary Notes:** Vegetarian, Gluten-Free

Wrenn was impressed with Teferi's creation. But she would bring something even better to their al fresco dining. She could commune with any root, stem, or vegetable to learn their scrumptious secrets, and her salad showcased the bounty of the Kessig wilds. Had Tibalt been asked to choose between the dishes, he would have called it a tie. (Yes, they invited him. No, don't question it.) He wanted to be on the good side of "Wrenferi." Who knows what that powerful pair could do?

Egg Salad Mixture

6 hard-boiled eggs

2 scallions, chopped

¼ cup mayo

1 tablespoon Dijon mustard

2 tablespoons sour cream

1 tablespoon lemon juice

Per Serving

½ cup romaine lettuce, roughly chopped

½ cup arugula, roughly chopped

¼ cup spinach, roughly chopped

10 to 15 mini tomatoes, cut in half

¼ cup broccoli, roughly chopped

10 sugar snap peas, cut in half

¼ yellow bell pepper, roughly chopped

¼ egg salad mixture

2 ounces blue cheese

Place the eggs in a pot and fill with enough water to cover completely. Cover with a lid and place over medium-high heat. Bring to a boil for 7 minutes.

Once the timer for the eggs has finished, immediately take the pot off the stove and place under cold running water. Move the eggs to a bowl with ice cubes and cold water and let sit for 3 minutes.

Carefully de-shell the eggs. Roughly chop the eggs and place in a medium bowl. Add the remaining ingredients and mix until combined. Season with salt and pepper.

Note: *This makes enough for 4 salad portions.*

Toss together the romaine lettuce, arugula, and spinach. Place in a medium bowl and lightly press down into a level layer.

Note: *A clear bowl is highly recommended for this salad. This will show off the colorful layers.*

Place a layer of tomatoes. If you don't have enough tomatoes to make a full layer, make sure to have the tomatoes near the outside of the bowl to show off the layers. You can fill the center with extra lettuce if needed.

Continue the layering process with a layer of broccoli, then sugar snap peas, and yellow bell peppers.

Top with egg salad and blue cheese.

AVACYN'S BIRTHDAY CAKE

Difficulty: ■■■□ • **Prep Time:** 1 hour • **Inactive Time:** 24 hours • **Cook Time:** 1 hour

Yield: 1 cake • **Dietary Notes:** Vegetarian

Tibalt loved angst, and Sorin and Avacyn were his leading actors. Vampire and Angel. Maker and Unmade. They were a team since the days of yore when everything with a claw, fang, or serrated blade was devouring hapless humans. Sorin created the archangel Avacyn to save the humans from extinction. With the power of her church, they stood against the forces of darkness. But in a turn of events that involved a multitude of tentacles, Sorin was forced to unmake her and send Avacyn back to the aether. He felt like he lost his daughter. Every year on the anniversary of her creation, he makes a black-and-white cake in remembrance of his angel.

Cherry Filling

2 tablespoons water

¼ cup sugar

3 tablespoons kirsch

1 lb cherries, pitted and cut in half

Chocolate Shards

5 ounces dark chocolate, chopped

Chocolate Cake

2 ½ cups cake flour

¾ cup cocoa powder

2 teaspoons instant coffee powder

1 tablespoon baking powder

1 teaspoon kosher salt

1 cup unsalted butter, room temperature

1 ½ cups sugar

2 whole eggs

2 egg whites

1 tablespoon vanilla paste

2 teaspoons kirsch

1 cup sour cream

½ cup heavy cream

Whipped Cream Frosting

3 cups heavy cream

1 tablespoon kirsch

1 teaspoon vanilla extract

1 tablespoon agar-agar

1 cup confectioners' sugar

Topping

Fresh cherries

Cherry Filling

The night before, combine water and sugar. Bring to a boil. Add kirsch and cherries. Reduce to a simmer and cook for 10 minutes.

Transfer to an airtight container and allow to cool. Let sit in the refrigerator at least overnight, up to 2 weeks.

Before using the cherries as a filling, place in a fine mesh strainer to remove excess syrup from the cherries.

Note: *This will help prevent the filling section from becoming too wet and causing the whipped cream to lose its volume.*

Chocolate Shards

The night before, place the chocolate in a microwave-safe bowl and microwave until it melts, about 45 seconds in total. Make sure to mix it a few times during the heating process so none of it burns.

Transfer the melted chocolate to a large sheet of parchment paper and spread out into a thin rectangle. Take the edge of the parchment paper and roll over the chocolate, making sure the chocolate is not touching. Place in the refrigerator until you are going to decorate.

Once ready to decorate, lightly press the paper to create a few cracks in the chocolate. Unroll completely to reveal the chocolate shards. Make sure to keep this cool to prevent the chocolate from melting.

Continued on next page

Chocolate Cake

Preheat an oven to 350°F. Prepare two 8-inch cake pans and spray the insides with nonstick spray. Carefully line each with parchment paper.

Combine the cake flour, cocoa powder, instant coffee powder, baking powder, and salt in a bowl and set aside. In a large bowl, combine the butter and sugar and mix until smooth. Add the eggs, egg whites, vanilla paste, and kirsch.

Add half of the dry ingredients into the large bowl and mix well. Add the sour cream and heavy cream. Mix until smooth. Add the remaining dry ingredients and mix until just combined.

Split the batter evenly between the two prepared cake pans. Lift each of the pans and bang lightly on the counter to remove any large air bubbles. Place in the oven and bake for 40 to 45 minutes, or until a toothpick test comes out clean.

Allow to rest for 5 minutes and then remove from the pan onto a cooling rack. Make sure to remove the parchment paper from the cakes and allow them to cool fully, at least 1 hour of resting time.

Whipped Cream Frosting

Combine heavy cream, kirsch, vanilla extract, agar-agar, and sugar in the bowl of a stand mixer set with the whisk attachment. Whip on high speed until medium peaks form. If you aren't ready to assemble the cake, cover the frosting bowl with plastic wrap and place in the refrigerator.

Topping

Once the cake layers have fully cooled, level both layers by cutting the top bump with a serrated knife. Brush the cut sides of the cake with the cherry syrup. Place one of the layers on your serving plate, cut side up.

Add about ½ inch of frosting on top and spread evenly. Add the cherry filling in the center, spreading it close to the edge but not completely. Cover the filling with additional frosting.

Top with the other layer of cake, cut side down. If you still have cherry syrup left, brush the top side with it.

Prepare a piping bag with a large round decorating tip. Transfer a small portion of the whipped cream frosting into the piping bag. Completely cover the cake with the remaining whipped cream frosting. To get nice smooth sides, position an offset spatula edge against the side and rotate the cake around.

Take the prepared piping bag and make little whipped cream dollops around the top of the cake. Take fresh cherries and place on top of each of the dollops. Carefully press the chocolate shards to the side of the cake. Let the cake sit covered in the refrigerator for at least 1 hour before cutting into it. It can be stored in the refrigerator for up to 4 days.

KALDHEIM

✦ ✦ ─────────── ✦ ─────────── ✦ ✦

Kaldheim is a plane of diverse realms all connected by the World Tree. From the vikings of Bretagard to the elves of Skemfar and the dwarves of Axgard, this is a land of hardy warriors who enjoy feasts and epic adventures in equal measure. Tyvar Kell should know: His journey started in Skemfar long before his spark ignited. Kaldheim is home to a family of gods who, despite their power, choose to walk among their people across the realms. It's not uncommon to see them drinking mead with their subjects and boasting about their greatest feats. The gods don't judge a warrior's worthiness. That is the job of the valkyries, proud battle angels who live in Starnheim, a divine realm at the top of the tree. Only those who earn their approval can enter the Hall of the Valkyries where the reveries never end. Gods were one thing, but the valkyries were Tyvar's primary concern.

There were only two ways to earn a valkyrie's blessing: either die victorious in battle or impress them with an *epic* feat. Tyvar was confident in his ability to put on a good show; he was the master of epic feats. He once turned seven rampaging trolls to stone all at the same time. He lassoed a twelve-legged stag and rode it across the lava fields of Surtland. He bested the Gold Dragon, stole his hoard, and distributed it among Kaldheim's realms. Each time he felt the valkyries' watchful eyes on him, but nothing earned him the invitation to dine in their hall. Then, a realization hit Tyvar harder than a hammer pounding forged metal. He had the feats part down, but he was missing the food. Determination swelling in his chest, Tyvar resolved to earn his seat at the table with glorious dishes even the divine eyes and stomachs of the valkyries couldn't refuse.

"Bough and Shadow" Bread

Difficulty: ■■■□□ • **Prep Time:** 45 minutes • **Inactive Time:** 25 hours • **Cook Time:** 1 hour 40 minutes
Yield: 1 loaf • **Dietary Notes:** Vegetarian, Dairy-Free

Tyvar loves to tell the saga of his brother, King Harald, who united all elves under his banner. The Wood and Shadow elves had fought for generations, and Harald was tired of it. Harald demanded both sides meet for a battle to determine who rules Skemfar once and for all. The Wood Elves arrived with their Jasper-bough bows, while the Shadow Elves wielded their shadow-infused blades. But Harald used powerful magic to transform the weapons into ingredients for delicious loaves. He fed both armies and ended their feud.

¼ cup sunflower seeds

¼ cup pumpkin seeds

¼ cup + 1 tablespoon flax seeds

¼ cup wheat berries

¼ cup rye berries

2 tablespoons millet

2 tablespoons white sesame seeds

2 tablespoons pearled barley

2 tablespoons oat bran

1 ¾ cups water, split

¾ cup dark rye flour

½ cup whole wheat flour

¾ cup bread flour

1 teaspoon active dry yeast

1 tablespoon kosher salt

1 ½ tablespoons unsulfured molasses

1 tablespoon honey

Combine the sunflower seeds, pumpkin seeds, flax seeds, wheat berries, rye berries, millet, sesame seeds, pearled barley, and oat bran in a medium bowl. Add 1 cup of water and stir together until well mixed. Cover and let rest at room temperature for 12 hours.

Combine the dark rye flour, wheat flour, bread flour, and yeast in a large bowl. Whisk together until combined. Add ¾ cup of water and mix until it just comes together. Place on a lightly floured surface and knead for about 2 minutes, until everything is homogeneous. The dough will be pretty dry at this point. Place back in the bowl, cover, and let rest at room temperature for 12 hours.

Transfer the flour mixture to the bowl of a stand mixer set with the paddle attachment. Add the soaked seeds, salt, molasses, and honey to the bowl. Mix at low speed for 10 minutes to knead the mixture together.

Note: *If you do not have a stand mixer, this can be done by hand. Keep in mind that the dough will be very sticky and wet. Keep your hands moist while working with this dough to prevent sticking.*

Once mixed, transfer to an oiled bowl and cover. Allow to rest at room temperature for 12 hours.

Prepare a 9-by-5-by-3-inch loaf pan with nonstick spray. Sprinkle with rye flour, coating the interior of the pan. Transfer the dough into the pan and smooth to level the top. Cover and allow to rest at room temperature for 1 hour.

Preheat oven to 350°F. Cover the pan with aluminum foil and bake for 1 hour. Uncover and bake for another 40 minutes, or until the bread is cooked through (an internal temperature of 200°F). Remove from the pan and allow to cool completely before cutting.

SKEMFAR'S BOUNTY

Difficulty: ■□□□□ • **Prep Time:** 20 minutes • **Inactive Time:** 2 hours • **Yield:** 6 - 8 servings • **Dietary Notes:** N/A

While Tyvar and Harald have had their brotherly disputes, they join forces when anything threatens Skemfar. A frost giant once tried to invade Skemfar, but Tyvar and Harald stopped him in his tracks. While Harald distracted him, Tyvar turned his legs to dandelions. Then he wrapped the frost giant up in honeysuckle vines and made a hammock for him in the branches above the river. The water began to freeze, and the fish jumped onto the shores where the elves were waiting. They celebrated their victory with a giant fish feast.

Smoked White Fish Dip

8 ounces cream cheese

4 ounces sour cream

2 scallions, chopped

¼ red onion, chopped

1 tablespoon horseradish

2 tablespoons lemon juice

1 teaspoon lemon zest

10 ounces smoked white fish

Per Serving

2 thin slices of "Bough and Shadow" Bread (page 107)

smoked white fish dip

pea sprouts

2 tablespoons tobiko

Smoked White Fish Dip

Whisk together the cream cheese and sour cream in a medium bowl.

Add the other ingredients and mix until just combined. Place in an airtight container and refrigerate for 2 hours before serving. Can be stored in the refrigerator for up to 1 week.

Per Serving

Top the "Bough and Shadow" Bread with a generous serving of the smoked white fish dip. Top with some pea sprouts and 1 tablespoon of tobiko. Serve immediately.

INFERNAL PET STEW

Difficulty: ■■☐☐☐ • **Prep Time:** 45 minutes • **Cook Time:** 4 hours • **Yield:** 4 - 6 servings • **Dietary Notes:** Gluten-Free

Tyvar had been to Immersturm once before with his friend, Kaya. It was a noxious, molten realm where demons aboard flaming longships delighted in destruction and mayhem. Tyvar wasn't keen to go back, but it was the only place where the main ingredient for Infernal Pet Stew could be obtained. The delicacy would surely impress the valkyries. The demons were infamous for their cruelty, but even they feared the Infernal Pets, who could turn a troll to ash in seconds. After a long search, Tyvar located a plump pet sunning itself in the glow of the magma with a large pile of demon bones next to it. He decided he'd use goat for his stew instead. There were other recipes that could earn him his glory.

1 lb goat, bone in, cut into chunks

canola oil

kosher salt

1 fennel bulb

2 carrots

½ green cabbage

5 cups chicken stock

½ ounce thyme sprigs

1 bay leaf

3 Yukon Gold potatoes, peeled and cut into chunks

Generously season the goat with salt. Heat a dutch oven over medium heat and add 1 tablespoon of canola oil. Add a single layer of the goat, being careful not to overcrowd the pan. Brown all sides of the meat. Remove and place on a plate. Add additional canola oil, if needed, and continue this process until all the goat has been browned.

Add another tablespoon of canola oil to the dutch oven. Add the fennel and carrots. Cook until the fennel has softened, about 5 minutes.

Add the cabbage and cook until it has slightly wilted, about 3 minutes. Add the chicken stock and goat meat. Mix until everything is combined.

Note: *If everything is not covered by the broth, keep in mind that as this cooks, the cabbage will wilt more and decrease in size.*

Add the thyme and bay leaf. Bring to a boil. Reduce the heat and keep at a lower simmer. Cover, keeping the lid slightly ajar, and cook for 3 hours, or until the goat meat is tender.

Once tender, add the potatoes and cook for another 30 minutes, or until the potatoes are firm but tender.

Cosmos Elixir

Difficulty: ■■☐☐☐ • **Prep Time:** 20 minutes • **Inactive Time:** 12 hours • **Cook Time:** 15 minutes
Yield: 6 servings • **Dietary Notes:** Vegetarian

Tyvar once challenged Halvar, God of Battle, to a wrestling match. Halvar had been raised by the dwarves of Axgard, and he was tougher than an ogre's jawbone. The two faced off in Istfell, the misty realm at the base of the World Tree. The "battle" lasted for three days, and as they tussled, they shook the foundations of Kaldheim. Halvar punched Tyvar so hard, he flew into Karfell. The draugrs looked more than surprised when an elf flew across their skies. But Tyvar bounced back by hitting him over the head with a kraken. When Halvar regained his wits, he conceded and offered Tyvar a drink from the Cosmos Elixir, a precious drink usually reserved for just the gods.

Apple Pie Simple Syrup

¼ cup honey

¼ cup water

1 cinnamon stick

2 cloves

2 allspice berries

2 cardamom pods

Cocktail

One 750-milliliter bottle mead

¼ cup vodka

1 cup apple cider

1 red apple, sliced

1 granny smith apple, sliced

2 lemons, sliced

Combine honey and water in a saucepan and place over medium-high heat. Mix together. Once the honey dissolves, add the cinnamon stick, cloves, allspice berries, and cardamom pods and bring to a simmer. Reduce the heat to medium-low and simmer for 20 minutes. Remove the whole spices and discard. Transfer the syrup to a pitcher and allow it to cool before adding the other ingredients.

Add the mead, vodka, and apple cider to the syrup pitcher and mix until combined. Add the apples and lemon. Refrigerate for at least 12 hours. Serve over ice with extra fruit if desired.

THE DOOMSKAR

Difficulty: ■☐☐☐☐ • **Prep Time:** 15 minutes • **Cook Time:** 25 minutes • **Yield:** 1 cocktail • **Dietary Notes:** Vegetarian, Dairy-Free

Tyvar had one last idea to impress the valkyries. He would race Toski, the giant squirrel, to the top of the World Tree. Toski could scurry from realm to realm with ease, and no one knew the tree better than him. Toski agreed that if Tyvar won the race, the squirrel would sneak him into Starnheim. But Tyvar had a magical trick up his sleeve, literally. A tumultuous event known as a Doomskar occurs when two realms collide. Tyvar had survived one recently, and he captured some of its incredible power in a rare liquid form. The race began, and Toski took an early lead. Tyvar exhaled, drank just a sip of Doomskar, and ROCKETED to the top of the World Tree with a speed that even Toski couldn't beat.

Rosemary Honey Syrup

½ cup honey

2 tablespoons sugar

½ cup water

3 rosemary sprigs

Per Cocktail

1 ounce rosemary honey syrup

1 ounce gin

2 ounces mead

1 ounce lemon juice

1 dash bitters

1 lemon peel

½ rosemary sprig

Ice

Rosemary Honey Syrup

Combine sugar, honey, and water in a saucepan and place over medium-high heat. Mix together. Once the sugar and honey dissolve, add the rosemary sprigs and bring to a simmer. Reduce the heat to medium-low and simmer for 25 minutes. Remove from the heat and let cool. Once cooled, cover, and store in the refrigerator for up to 2 weeks.

Per Cocktail

Fill a cocktail shaker with ice. Add rosemary honey syrup, gin, mead, lemon juice, and bitters. Shake thoroughly for 15 seconds. Pour through a mesh strainer into a glass with fresh ice cubes, a lemon peel, and rosemary sprig.

"Eternal Feast" Roast

Difficulty: ■■■□ • **Prep Time:** 1 hour • **Inactive Time:** 12 hours • **Cook Time:** 30 minutes
Yield: 6 - 8 servings • **Dietary Notes:** Dairy-Free

To Tyvar's surprise, the gates of Starnheim were open when he reached the top of the World Tree. He bade Toski farewell and headed to the Hall of the Valkyries. Two valkyries appeared and hovered above him. Their golden wings flashed in the rainbow light, and they raised their weapons to smite him for his audacity. Tyvar slipped a bag off his shoulder and knelt down. He opened the bag and revealed all the ingredients to make a feast for the valkyries. No one had ever cooked for the mighty angels before! They were so surprised—and pleased—that they escorted him inside the grand hall, where he immediately started preparing a roast suitable for the glory of Starnheim.

2 racks of lamb

1 ½ tablespoons coriander seeds

1 tablespoon mustard seeds

½ tablespoon fennel seeds

1 tablespoon juniper berries

1 tablespoon kosher salt

2 teaspoons ground black pepper

2 fresh thyme sprigs, stems removed
and leaves chopped

1 fresh rosemary sprig, stems removed
and leaves chopped

5 garlic cloves, chopped

2 tablespoons olive oil

Tyvar's Pilaf (page 121)

butcher twine

Prepare the racks of lamb by placing the lamb on a cutting board, fat side down. Make a shallow cut in between each of the ribs to help with shaping the crown. Transfer to a wire rack on a baking sheet.

Place the coriander seeds, mustard seeds, and fennel seeds in a stainless-steel pan. Heat over medium-high heat to toast the spices. Cook until toasted, about 3 minutes. Transfer to a spice grinder and add the juniper berries. Grind into a fine powder.

Combine the ground spices, salt, pepper, thyme, rosemary, garlic, and olive oil. Rub the racks of lamb until fully coated. Place in the refrigerator and marinate for at least 4 hours, up to 12 hours.

Remove the lamb from the refrigerator to make the crown. Place both of the racks next to each other, fat side up. Tie the two bones that are next to each other together with kitchen twine. Stand the racks up so the bones are facing up.

Shape into a crown, with the fat side facing inward. Tie together the other side that is now touching. Take more twine and wrap it around the bottom to help tighten the crown together. Cut off any excess twine. To help hold the shape, place the crown in a Bundt pan, with the bones facing up. Let rest at room temperature for 45 minutes.

Preheat oven to 450°F. Place the lamb in the oven and roast until the meat reaches the desired temperature:

> **Medium-Rare:** *125°F - 25 minutes*
> **Medium:** *135°F - 30 minutes*
> **Medium-Well:** *140°F - 35 minutes*

Remove from the oven and cover in aluminum foil. Let rest for 10 minutes. To serve, remove the kitchen twine and fill the center of the rack with Tyvar's Pilaf.

TOSKI'S MEDLEY

Difficulty: ■■□□□ • **Prep Time:** 20 minutes • **Cook Time:** 1 hour • **Yield:** 6 servings • **Dietary Notes:** Vegan

Toski was scampering down the tree when the scent of roasting lamb reached him. He was so pleased that Tyvar had survived the encounter with the valkyries that he returned to Starnheim to contribute his own dish. He brought potatoes from a garden in Bretagard and wild carrots from the Gnottvold forests. He added in the finest fennel from misty Littjara and parsnips grown around the hot springs of Surtland. Everyone loved Toski's squirrel-approved medley, which brought a taste of many realms to the valkyries' table.

2 lbs Yukon Gold potatoes, quartered

3 parsnips, cut into 1-inch pieces

3 carrots, cut into 1-inch pieces

1 fennel bulb, sliced

4 shallots, sliced

3 tablespoons olive oil

5 thyme sprigs

2 teaspoons kosher salt

1 teaspoon ground black pepper

Preheat oven to 400°F. Place the potatoes, parsnips, carrots, fennel, and shallots in a large bowl with olive oil. Toss until all the vegetables are coated.

Prepare a baking sheet with aluminum foil and nonstick spray. Place the thyme sprigs on the baking sheet. Transfer the oiled vegetables onto the baking sheet and season with salt and pepper. Place in the oven and bake for 1 hour, tossing every 20 minutes.

TYVAR'S PILAF

Difficulty: ■■■□□ • **Prep Time:** 30 minutes • **Cook Time:** 45 minutes • **Yield:** 6 servings • **Dietary Notes:** Vegetarian

In addition to the roast and Toski's Medley, Tyvar cooked a delicious pilaf made with barley harvested from the base of the World Tree in Istfell. As the valkyries enjoyed the incredible meal, Tyvar felt more satisfied with his creation than any act of derring-do he had performed before. At long last, he enjoyed a raucous evening with the legends of Kaldheim in glory and celebration.

1 cup pearl barley

2 ½ cups vegetable broth

1 bay leaf

½ cinnamon stick

2 teaspoons kosher salt

3 tablespoons unsalted butter

2 leeks, white and light green parts, chopped

1 fennel bulb, sliced

6 garlic cloves, chopped

1 tablespoon dried thyme

2 teaspoons dried sage

½ teaspoon ground black pepper

Combine the barley, vegetable broth, bay leaf, cinnamon stick, and 1 teaspoon salt in a medium pot. Place over medium-high heat and bring to a boil. Reduce the heat and simmer with the lid on for 30 minutes, or until the liquid is absorbed. Remove from the heat and let rest, covered, for 10 minutes. Discard the bay leaf and cinnamon stick.

In a large nonstick pan over medium-high heat, melt the butter. Add the leeks, fennel, and garlic and cook until softened, about 8 minutes. Add the thyme, sage, 1 teaspoon salt, and pepper. Toss to coat well. Add the barley and mix together until completely coated. Season with additional salt and pepper to your liking.

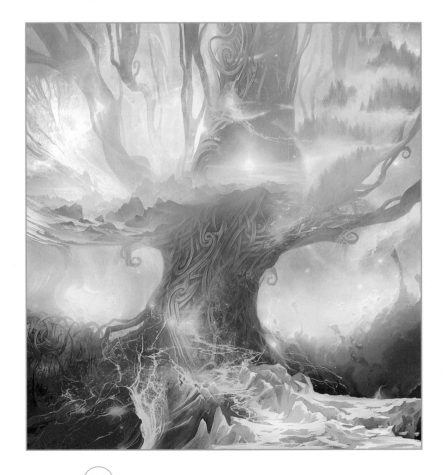

KAMIGAWA

◆ ┄ ◆ ─────────────────────── ◆ ┄ ◆

Kamigawa has struggled to balance modernity and tradition for generations. This conflict touches all areas of life, from magic to politics to culinary techniques. Tamiyo could spend the day in the countryside with denizens who follow old traditions and be in a city full of high-tech innovations later that evening. Kamigawa was also home to spirits known as kami. While Kamigawa's Imperial Court sets official policy, other factions have different philosophies regarding the kami, cultural practices, and the technological revolution.

Tamiyo loved every part of Kamigawa, including the rough edges it was still figuring out how to smooth. But she also craved knowledge and traveled the Multiverse to find stories from every plane. How had other worlds reconciled innovation and identity? What lessons could she learn from these far-flung planes? She recorded these stories in her notebooks, where they became spells of great power. She carried her notebooks with her on her travels with one exception. A special book remained on the shelf in her kitchen. Her husband, Genku, and their children were welcome and encouraged to use it while she was away. Instead of spells, this notebook contained recipes she used to teach her children something important about their world.

Tamiyo believed wholeheartedly that knowledge should be shared, so a lesson often accompanied dinner. The family would prepare the meal together. Then they lit candles and sat down together. Over the meal, they discussed all manner of things, such as history, or kami magic, or the meaning of life.

TAMIYO'S GIFT

Difficulty: ■■■□ • **Prep Time:** 2 hours • **Inactive Time:** 12 hours • **Cook Time:** 1 hour
Yield: 6 of each type • **Dietary Notes:** Dairy-Free

The nightly meal was Tamiyo's gift to her family and a precious time to appreciate innovation and tradition right in her own home. This is Tamiyo's signature dish, which she has often shared with friends and family. Those who have enjoyed the dish swear it has magical properties: It never fails to spark lively discussions, conjure happy memories, and craft bonds among those around the table.

Spicy Tuna

10 ounces tuna

kosher salt

ground black pepper

1 scallion, sliced

2 tablespoons Japanese mayo

1 tablespoon gochujang

1 teaspoon ichimi togarashi

3 cups sushi rice

water (follow your rice cooker's directions)

2 tablespoons rice vinegar

1 tablespoon sugar

½ teaspoon salt

Spicy Tuna

Season the tuna with salt and pepper on all sides. Spray a pan with nonstick spray and place over medium-high heat. Sauté the tuna until each side turns golden and the fish is cooked through, about 6 to 8 minutes. Remove from the heat.

Shred the tuna and place in a bowl. Add the scallion, Japanese mayo, gochujang, and ichimi togarashi and stir until combined. Set aside until the rice is cooked.

Spicy Tuna Assembly

Put rice in a bowl, fill it up with cold water, and rub in a circular motion. The water will become opaque, which means the rice still needs to be cleaned. Strain the water out and repeat until the water is clear.

Place the cleaned rice and the amount of water required into a rice cooker and allow the rice to cook.

When the rice is done cooking, remove from the rice cooker and place inside a non-metallic bowl.

In a small bowl, combine rice vinegar, sugar, and salt. Add the vinegar mixture to the rice while the rice is still hot. Take a rice paddle and fold in the rice vinegar. Continue to fold and slice the rice until it has cooled down. Cover with a wet towel to keep the rice nice and moist.

Continued on next page

Salt Salmon

½ lb salmon, cut into four portions

1 tablespoon sake

1 teaspoon soy sauce

1 ½ tablespoons salt

1 scallion, sliced

3 cups sushi rice

water (follow your rice cooker's
    directions)

2 tablespoons rice vinegar

1 tablespoon sugar

½ teaspoon salt

¼ cup furikake

2 tablespoons white sesame seeds

2 tablespoons black sesame seeds

Tobiko

2 ½ cups sushi rice

½ cup black rice

water (follow your rice cooker's
    directions)

2 tablespoons rice vinegar

1 tablespoon sugar

½ teaspoon salt

6 ounces tobiko

To assemble the onigiri, split the rice into 6 portions. Take half of one of the portions and place on a large sheet of plastic wrap. Shape into a disc with a deep divot in the center. Place one-sixth of the tuna filling in that divot, but don't overfill. Too much filling will make it more difficult to shape the rice ball.

Note: *When working with the sushi rice, it is extremely important that you keep your hands moist. Keep a bowl of water nearby.*

Top with the other half of the rice and seal in the filling, shaping into a rough ball. Wrap with the plastic wrap and place a moderate amount of pressure to shape into a triangle. If you are not eating this immediately, keep it wrapped in the plastic wrap and place in the refrigerator. These can be stored in the refrigerator for up to 1 week.

Repeat until all onigiri are formed. Serve with a piece of nori.

Salt Salmon

The night before, rub the salmon with the sake and soy sauce and let rest for 5 minutes. Pat the salmon dry and salt the salmon on all sides. Prepare an airtight container with a paper towel at the bottom. Place the salmon on top in a single layer. Cover with another paper towel and seal the airtight container. Let rest in the refrigerator for at least 12 hours and up to 24 hours.

Pat dry and place on a baking sheet. Place under a broiler and cook for 3 minutes. Flip and cook for another 3 minutes, until both sides are crispy. Remove from the oven and allow to cool. Remove the skin and transfer the rest to a bowl. Toss together with the scallions. Set aside until the rice is cooked.

Salt Salmon Assembly

Put rice in a bowl, fill it up with cold water, and rub in a circular motion. The water will become opaque, which means the rice still needs to be cleaned. Strain the water out and repeat until the water is clear.

Place the cleaned rice and the amount of water required into a rice cooker and allow the rice to cook.

When the rice is done cooking, remove from the rice cooker and place inside a non-metallic bowl.

In a small bowl, combine rice vinegar, sugar, and salt. Add the vinegar mixture to the rice while the rice is still hot. Take a rice paddle and fold in the rice vinegar. Continue to fold and slice the rice until it has cooled down.

Add the furikake and sesame seeds and mix until just combined. Cover with a wet towel to keep the rice nice and moist.

To assemble the onigiri, split the rice into 6 portions. Take half of one of the portions and place on a large sheet of plastic wrap. Shape into a disc with a deep divot in the center. Place one-sixth of the salted salmon filling in the divot, but don't overfill. Too much filling will make it more difficult to shape the rice ball.

Note: *When working with the sushi rice, it is extremely important that you keep your hands moist. Keep a bowl of water nearby.*

Top with the other half of the rice and seal in the filling, shaping into a rough ball. Wrap with the plastic wrap and place a moderate amount of pressure to shape into a triangle. If you are not eating this immediately, keep it wrapped in the plastic wrap and place in the refrigerator. These can be stored in the refrigerator for up to 1 week.

Repeat until all onigiri are formed.

Tobiko Assembly

Put the sushi rice in a bowl and fill it with cold water. With your hands, rub in a circular motion. You'll notice the water is opaque, which means the rice still needs to be cleaned. Strain the water out and repeat until the water is clear. Place the cleaned sushi rice, black rice, and water required into a rice cooker and allow the combined rice to cook.

When the rice is done cooking, remove from the rice cooker and place inside a non-metallic bowl.

In a small bowl, combine rice vinegar, sugar, and salt. Add the vinegar mixture to the rice while the rice is still hot. Take a rice paddle and fold in the rice vinegar. Continue to fold and slice the rice until it has cooled down. Cover with a wet towel to keep the rice nice and moist.

To assemble the onigiri, split the rice into 6 portions. Take half of one of the portions and place on a large sheet of plastic wrap. Shape into a disc with a deep divot in the center. Place 1 ounce of tobiko in that divot, but don't overfill. Too much filling will make it more difficult to shape the rice ball.

Note: *When working with the sushi rice, it is extremely important that you keep your hands moist. Keep a bowl of water nearby.*

Top with the other half of the rice and seal in the filling, shaping into a rough ball. Wrap with the plastic wrap and place a moderate amount of pressure to shape into a triangle. If you are not eating this immediately, keep it wrapped in the plastic wrap and place in the refrigerator. These can be stored in the refrigerator for up to 1 week.

Repeat until all onigiri are formed.

IMPERIAL RAMEN

Difficulty: ■■■■■ · **Prep Time:** 1 hour · **Inactive Time:** 24 hours · **Cook Time:** 7 hours
Yield: 6 servings · **Dietary Notes:** Dairy-Free

Shortly after Tamiyo returned from Ravnica, her family selected a recipe for Imperial Ramen from her book. Like the Imperial Court, the dish had many layers, and it took time to understand its complexities. Tamiyo told her children about the Emperor, who had been missing for years. As they cut vegetables, she told them about Kyodai, the dragon spirit who dwells at the court. While broth simmered, they talked about how power can be both a blessing and a curse, like a stove. Too much heat, and the soup will boil over and be ruined. But without the stove, they wouldn't have warm food or heat on cold nights. As they enjoyed the meal together, they expressed their gratitude for the court (and the stove) and the stability it provided.

Miso Ajitsuke Tamago

Note: *These are a completely optional part of the recipe. The broth for this can be very heavy and the addition of the egg might be too much for some.*

6 eggs

½ cup soy sauce

2 tablespoons light brown sugar

2 tablespoons shiro miso

¼ cup mirin

¼ cup sake

Poultry Paitan

1 whole duck, broken down and skin
    from breast region reserved for oil

1 whole chicken, broken down and skin
    from breast region reserved for oil

1 lb chicken feet, claws removed

1 head of garlic, cut in half

One 3-inch piece of ginger, sliced

4 scallions, cut in half

Garlic Duck Oil

⅓ cup canola oil

duck skin, reserved from broth

chicken skin, reserved from broth

6 garlic cloves, minced

Miso Ajitsuke Tamago

Bring a pot of water to a boil. Gently place the eggs in the pot, cover, and cook for 6 ½ minutes. Once cooked, immediately take the pot off the stove and place the eggs under cold running water. Move the eggs to a bowl with ice cubes and water. Carefully remove the shells from the eggs.

Mix the soy sauce, sugar, miso, mirin, and sake in a sealable bag. Add the eggs. Seal and make sure the eggs are fully covered. Place in the refrigerator and marinate for at least 24 hours. Can be stored in the refrigerator for up to 3 days.

Poultry Paitan

Place the duck, chicken, and chicken feet in a large pot. Cover with enough water to just cover. Place over medium-high heat and bring to a boil. Skim off any scum that forms at the top.

Keep this at a rolling boil and add additional water as it reduces during 4 hours of cooking. Make sure to smash the meat and bones a few times, about every 30 minutes or so.

After the 4 hours have passed, add the garlic and ginger to the pot. Allow to boil for another 1 ½ hours. At this point, do not add any more water to the pot and continue to smash the meat and bones from time to time.

Add the scallions and cook for another 30 minutes.

After the cook time has passed, transfer to a large bowl through a fine mesh strainer. Press the bones and meat in the strainer to get all of the broth into the bowl. Discard everything in the mesh strainer. If you are making the ramen immediately after, keep the broth warm. If serving the next day, transfer to an airtight container and allow to cool completely before storing in the refrigerator.

Continued on next page

Miso Tare

One 1-inch piece ginger, grated

3 garlic cloves, grated

¼ cup aka miso

⅓ cup shiro miso

½ cup sake

2 tablespoons soy sauce

1 tablespoon mirin

½ teaspoon monosodium glutamate

1 tablespoon kosher salt

2 teaspoons brown sugar

Poached Chicken

2 chicken breasts

¼ onion, sliced

One 2-inch piece of ginger, sliced

5 garlic cloves

1 bay leaf

½ chicken bouillon cube (6 g)

10 black peppercorns

2 Sichuan peppercorns

Toppings Per Serving

canola oil

1 king oyster mushroom, sliced

2 cups poultry paitan, warmed

1 to 2 tablespoons miso tare

2 teaspoons garlic duck oil

5 ounces ramen noodles, cooked

handful pea sprouts

2 tablespoons negi, white and
  light green parts, thinly sliced

3 slices narutomaki

3 to 5 slices poached chicken

1 miso ajitsuke tamago, cut in half

Note: *Keep in mind that the broth may split and have a fat layer at the top after sitting in the refrigerator. To fix this, when heating the broth up, make sure to whisk together well.*

Garlic Duck Oil

Place the canola oil, duck skin, and chicken skin in a saucepan over medium heat. Bring to a simmer, reduce the heat to medium-low, and allow to simmer for about 20 minutes. Keep an eye on this and do not allow the oil to burn.

Add the garlic and continue to simmer until it browns, about 10 minutes. Remove the skin and transfer to an airtight container. This can be stored in the refrigerator for 1 month.

Miso Tare

Combine everything in a saucepan. Place over medium heat and bring to a simmer. Lightly simmer for 10 minutes. Allow to cool and transfer to an airtight container. This can be stored in the refrigerator for 1 month.

Poached Chicken

Place the chicken breast, onion, ginger, garlic, bay leaf, chicken bouillon, and peppercorns in a small pot. Fill with water until the chicken is covered. Place over medium-high heat and bring to a boil. Lower heat to low and allow the chicken to simmer for 10 to 15 minutes, until the chicken registers an internal temperature of 165°F. Remove the chicken from the water and set aside to cool.

Toppings Per Serving

Heat a nonstick pan with 1 tablespoon of canola oil over medium-high heat. Add the king oyster mushrooms and panfry until golden brown, about 5 to 8 minutes per side. Set aside.

To set up a bowl of ramen, take a bowl and place 1 tablespoon of tare and the duck oil at the bottom. Add the paitan. Taste and add an additional tablespoon of tare if the broth is not salty enough for your liking.

Place the cooked ramen noodles in the center. Top with the cooked king oyster mushrooms, sprouts, negi, narutomaki, and chicken slices. Serve immediately with the ajitsuke tamago on the side.

STORMWATCHER'S DELIGHT

Difficulty: ■■□□□ • **Prep Time:** 45 minutes • **Cook Time:** 30 minutes • **Yield:** 6 servings • **Dietary Notes:** Dairy-Free

One day, as Tamiyo and her children walked along the river, the wind picked up, and the clouds moved quickly across the sky. Rumiyo asked if there were clouds in the skies of all worlds. Tamiyo said that many had them, but not all. The fast-moving clouds reminded Tamiyo of a plane she had visited many years earlier. She had been strolling through an open-air market when the weather turned stormy. The vendors invited her into their tent to enjoy a hot meal and watch the storm. The delicious dish—with its black rice—reminded her of the storm clouds on the horizon. When Tamiyo and her children returned from their walk, Tamiyo re-created the dish from memory, and they enjoyed it while watching the summer storm. It became a family favorite, and from then on, they called it Stormwatcher's Delight.

Black Rice

3 cups rice, cooked

½ cup black rice

water (follow the instructions of your rice cooker)

Gyudon

2 tablespoons sugar

1 tablespoon ichimi togarashi

1 tablespoon wasabi

One 2-inch piece of ginger

6 garlic cloves, minced

1 ½ cups beef stock

3 tablespoons soy sauce

2 tablespoons sake

3 tablespoons mirin

3 tablespoons kimchi juice

canola oil

2 king oyster mushrooms, sliced

1 ½ onions, thinly sliced

2 lbs ribeye steaks, very thinly sliced

Per Serving

cooked black rice

kimchi, sliced

kizami nori

beni shoga

black sesame seeds

Black Rice

Place the rice, black rice, and water in a rice cooker. Follow the instructions on your rice cooker and cook the rice.

Gyudon

Combine the sugar, ichimi togarashi, wasabi, ginger, garlic, beef stock, soy sauce, sake, mirin, and kimchi juice in a medium bowl and set aside.

Heat a medium pot with 1 tablespoon of canola oil over medium-high heat. Add the king oyster mushrooms and panfry until golden brown, about 5 to 8 minutes, per side. Add the onions and cook until softened, another 5 minutes.

Add the broth mixture and bring to a boil. Reduce the heat to low and allow the sauce to simmer for 5 minutes. Add the ribeye. Simmer for 5 to 8 minutes, or until the meat is just cooked.

Assembly

To serve, place ½ cup of cooked rice in a bowl and top with the gyudon. Pour a small amount of the sauce over the beef. Top with kimchi, kizami nori, beni shoga, and black sesame seeds.

SCRAPPERS' YAKISOBA

Difficulty: ■■□□□ • **Prep Time:** 30 minutes • **Cook Time:** 30 minutes • **Yield:** 6 - 8 servings • **Dietary Notes:** Vegan

It was too hot for cooking, so Tamiyo and her family walked to the market to buy dinner from one of their favorite stalls. The stall of choice was run by a woman from Sokenzanshi, and the children always ordered Scrappers' Yakisoba. Hiroku wondered aloud why such delicious noodles had that name. With dinner acquired, they sat on a bench together and talked about freedom and communalism between bites of saucy noodles. They postulated what it would be like not to have enough of the things they needed. Many of the Uprisers' creations, like the Scrappers' Yakisoba, were born out of ingenuity.

Spicy Yakisoba Sauce

1 tablespoon sake

2 tablespoons mirin

1 tablespoon soy sauce

1 tablespoon rice vinegar

2 tablespoons tonkatsu sauce

1 tablespoon worcestershire sauce

2 tablespoons chili paste

2 tablespoons honey

1 tablespoon ketchup

1 ½ tablespoon ichimi togarashi

1 tablespoon palm sugar

Yakisoba

canola oil

½ red onion, sliced

½ carrot, julienned

2 shiitake mushrooms, sliced

1 king oyster mushroom, sliced

½ cup kimchi, sliced

2 scallions, cut into 2-inch pieces

16 ounces yakisoba noodles, defrosted

Whisk together the ingredients for the yakisoba sauce.

Note: *If you want to reduce how spicy this sauce is, reduce the gochujang and ichimi togarashi.*

Heat a pan over medium-high heat with 1 tablespoon of canola oil. Add the onion, carrots, and mushrooms. Cook until the vegetables have softened, about 7 minutes. Add the kimchi and scallions, cook for another 5 minutes.

Place the yakisoba noodles in a colander and run under hot water to separate the noodles. Add the noodles to the pan and mix with the vegetables.

Add the yakisoba sauce and toss until completely coated.

BOSEIJU SHIRA-AE

Difficulty: ■■◻◻◻ • **Prep Time:** 30 minutes • **Inactive Time:** 1 hour • **Cook Time:** 15 minutes
Yield: 6 servings • **Dietary Notes:** Vegan

Tamiyo and her children ate lunch beneath Boseiju, the oldest tree on Kamigawa. It was a long journey, and they were happy when they found a secluded resting spot. The massive branches sheltered them, and they could no longer see the skyscrapers and glowing lights of the city. Tamiyo laid out food special to the Jukai Naturalists, and as they ate, she began the lesson. This dish was originally created under the boughs of the Boseiju. Tamiyo believes it's best enjoyed outdoors with the sound of the wind singing through the leaves of the ancient tree.

8 ounces firm tofu

1 bunch mizuna, bottoms removed

canola oil

1 carrot, shredded and julienned

1 bunch shimeji mushrooms, bottoms removed

1 tablespoon + 1 teaspoon soy sauce, split

3 teaspoons sake, split

3 tablespoons sesame seeds, toasted

½ cup edamame seeds, warmed

1 tablespoon sugar

1 teaspoon shiro miso

Wrap the tofu in a paper towel. Place between two plates and top with a heavy object. Allow to rest for 30 minutes in order to remove excess liquid. Remove the paper towel and wrap again in a new paper towel. Place back under the heavy object and rest for another 30 minutes.

Heat a pot of water over high heat and bring to a boil. Prepare a bowl with cold water and ice. Place the mizuna in the pot and boil for 1 minute. Transfer to the bowl with the ice water and let sit for 3 minutes.

Take the mizuna and squeeze out the excess water. Roughly chop into large chunks. Set aside.

Heat a nonstick pan with 1 tablespoon canola oil over medium-high heat. Add the carrots and sauté for 3 minutes. Add the shimeji mushrooms and cook until softened, about 3 minutes. Add 1 tablespoon soy sauce and 2 teaspoons of sake. Cook until the mushrooms have absorbed the liquid. Remove from the heat and set aside.

Place the sesame seeds in a mortar and pestle and press until half of them are broken. Transfer to a large bowl. Crumble the tofu into the bowl. Add the remaining soy sauce and sake, sugar, and shiro miso. Lightly mash until it comes together.

Add the mizuna, carrot, shimeji mushrooms, and edamame. Toss until combined. Serve immediately. Can be stored in an airtight container in the refrigerator for up to 3 days.

NATURALIST'S NASU DENGAKU

Difficulty: ■■□□□ • **Prep Time:** 30 minutes • **Cook Time:** 15 minutes • **Yield:** 6 servings • **Dietary Notes:** Vegan

They finished their meal with a second dish perfected by the Jukai. As they enjoyed the miso-glazed eggplant, they discussed the kami of the forest, wind, and earth, intent on understanding how they influenced the world. The family talked about the interconnectedness of all things, from the ants attempting to climb onto their lunch dishes to the sunshine nourishing the plants around them. Soon the lesson and the meal ended, but they all sat in hushed silence, thankful that the Boseiju persisted despite all that had changed.

Miso Glaze

¼ cup shiro miso

1 tablespoon sugar

½ tablespoon brown sugar

½ tablespoon mirin

2 tablespoons sake

Eggplant

4 Japanese eggplants

olive oil

toasted black sesame seeds

2 scallions, chopped

Whisk together all of the ingredients for the miso glaze and set aside.

Cut the eggplants in half lengthwise. If your eggplants are extremely long, cut the halves in half. Score the insides of the eggplants. Rub all parts of the eggplant with olive oil.

Heat a pan over medium-high heat. Place the cut side of the eggplant down on the pan and cover. Cook for 3 to 5 minutes, until slightly golden brown. Flip, cover, and cook for another 3 minutes. The eggplant should be slightly softened at this point. Transfer to a baking sheet, cut side up. Repeat this step until all the eggplant is cooked.

Brush the tops of the eggplants with the miso glaze. Place under a broiler and cook until caramelized, about 3 to 5 minutes. To serve, top with black sesame seeds and scallions.

KAITO'S MOCHI

Difficulty: ■ ■ ■ ■ ■   •   **Prep Time:** 1 ½ hours   •   **Inactive Time:** 2 hours   •   **Cook Time:** 5 minutes
Yield: 10 mochi   •   **Dietary Notes:** Gluten-Free, Dairy-Free, Vegetarian

While she had hoped it would be a long time before her family would be students of grief, Tamiyo sadly met a bitter fate at the hands of the Phyrexians. In her last days on Kamigawa, she scrawled down two recipes that her children found later. These dishes were inspired by other planeswalkers she met on her many travels, and she wanted to use them as a lesson about allies and enemies. Tamiyo wrote this about her friendship with Kaito Shizuki:

He is a trusted ally. Clever and thoughtful, but he hasn't lost the sense of joy he had as a child. These treats were his favorite. One day, he and the Emperor will share them again, here on Kamigawa.

Sesame Filling

½ cup black sesame seeds

¼ cup honey

⅔ cup shiroan

pinch of salt

Blue Mochi

1 ¼ cups shiratamako

1 tablespoon spirulina powder

⅓ cup sugar

1 cup water

potato starch

Sesame Filling

Heat the black sesame seeds in a stainless-steel pan over medium heat. Heat and stir often until they become fragrant, about 3 minutes. Remove from the heat and allow to cool.

Transfer to a spice grinder or mortar and pestle and grind into a powder. Transfer to a bowl. Combine with honey, shiroan, and salt. Mix until combined. Cover and place in the freezer for 30 minutes.

Prepare a plate with parchment paper and a bowl with water. Split the sesame filling into 10 equal portions (about 35 grams each). Wet your hands and take one of the portions. Shape into a ball and place on the parchment paper. Repeat until all the portions are prepared.

Place in the refrigerator until you are ready to fill the mochi.

Blue Mochi

Place the shiratamako, spirulina powder, and sugar in a microwave-safe bowl. Add the water and whisk until combined and there are no clumps.

Cover the bowl with a paper towel and place in the microwave for 30 seconds. Remove and whisk. Cover and place back in the microwave and heat for 1 minute. Remove and mix together, this time with a spatula because the mixture is beginning to thicken. Cover and place back in the microwave for another minute. Remove and mix once more. Cover and microwave for 30 more seconds.

Prepare a baking sheet with a piece of parchment paper and a generous layer of potato starch. Transfer the mochi mixture on top. Dust your hands with potato starch. Lightly press the dough out into a rectangle. Place in the refrigerator to rest for 15 minutes.

Note: *The dough is extremely sticky, so it is very important to keep your hands dusted with potato starch while working with it from here on.*

Prepare another plate with parchment paper and set aside. Split the dough into 10 portions. Take one of the portions and press into a 4-inch circle. Take one of the sesame balls and place it in the center. Pinch the mochi dough around the filling to seal. Lightly roll the sealed mochi in your hands to seal the bottom. Place on the plate covered with parchment paper, seal side down. Repeat until all the mochi have been formed.

Place in the refrigerator to rest for 1 hour before serving. Best enjoyed the same day.

FUTURIST OBANYAKI

Difficulty: ■■■□□ • **Prep Time:** 30 minutes • **Inactive Time:** 1 hour • **Cook Time:** 10 minutes per batch
Yield: 7 obanyaki • **Dietary Notes:** Vegetarian

Tamiyo's recipe for obanyaki gave her the perfect opportunity to discuss the Futurists with her children. The Futurists value technological innovation. They want to break with traditions and seek out new horizons. Tradition dictated that the pastry be a particular shape. But Tamiyo encouraged her children to experiment with new shapes. As they worked, they discussed creativity and responsibility. In the end, some of the shapes worked and some did not, but that was part of the process. Tamiyo made careful notes for her children in the book, so they could remember what they had learned for the next time.

Sweet Potato Filling

16 ounces sweet potatoes

2 to 3 tablespoons sweetened
    condensed milk

1 teaspoon vanilla extract

1 teaspoon kosher salt

2 teaspoons brown sugar

4 ounces mozzarella,
    cut into small cubes

Batter

1 ½ cups all-purpose flour

½ cup cake flour

2 teaspoons baking powder

pinch of salt

2 eggs

1 tablespoon sugar

1 tablespoon honey

1 teaspoon vanilla extract

1 ⅓ cups milk

Sweet Potato Filling

Preheat oven to 425°F. Place the sweet potatoes on an aluminum-lined baking sheet. Bake for 40 to 60 minutes, until the sweet potatoes are tender and can be easily pierced with a knife.

Note: *The bake time will depend on the size of the sweet potatoes. If the ones you are using are different sizes, make sure to check each.*

Remove the sweet potatoes from the oven and allow to cool until they are cool enough to work with. Remove the skins and discard. Smash the sweet potato and add the sweetened condensed milk, vanilla extract, salt, and sugar. Taste and adjust the sweetness level to your liking.

Add the cubed mozzarella and mix until well combined. Cover and allow the mixture to rest in the refrigerator for 1 hour.

Batter

Combine the flours, baking powder, and salt in a medium bowl. Whisk together the eggs, sugar, honey, and vanilla extract in a large bowl. Add half of the dry ingredients to the large bowl and whisk together.

Add the milk and whisk together well. Add the remaining dry ingredients and whisk until the batter just comes together. Set aside and let rest for 15 minutes. Transfer to a measuring cup with a spout for easier pouring.

Heat an obanyaki pan over medium-low heat. Lightly grease 2 of the 4 holes in the pan. Add the batter and fill halfway up. Allow to cook for 2 minutes, or until the sides begin to lightly bubble.

Take a generous tablespoon of the filling and place in the center of the pancake. Lightly grease the remaining holes in the pan and fill halfway up with batter. Cook for another 3 minutes.

Use a small, thin metal spatula to remove a pancake with the filling. Carefully flip it and place it on top of an unfilled pancake. Repeat this with the other filled pancake. Lightly press down and allow to cook for another 2 minutes. Remove from the pan and serve immediately. Repeat these steps until all the batter is used.

"REMEMBRANCE" NIKUDANGO

Difficulty: ■■□□□ • **Prep Time:** 20 minutes • **Inactive Time:** 20 minutes • **Cook Time:** 30 minutes
Yield: 16 nikudango • **Dietary Notes:** Dairy-Free

On the last page of her book, Tamiyo wrote down a story that she'd told her children many times over dinner. In the story, a monster invades a peaceful village. The village rallies together and slays the monster, but the village is destroyed, and many lose their lives in the battle. That last time they discussed the story over a delicious serving of meatballs, Tamiyo asked her children what they thought about it. Hiroku and Rumiyo said it saddened them, but Nashi said it was a hopeful story. He said: Even if bad things happen, you can endure. *Tamiyo agreed. She hugged her children and said:* No matter what happens, our family endures.

Nikudango

olive oil

2 shallots, minced

1 lb ground wild boar

One 2-inch piece of ginger, grated

1 tablespoon mirin

2 teaspoons soy sauce

1 teaspoon fish sauce

3 tablespoons potato starch

canola oil

Sauce

2 tablespoons soy sauce

1 tablespoon sake

2 tablespoons tonkatsu sauce

1 tablespoon honey

1 tablespoon rice vinegar

1 tablespoon potato starch

2 tablespoons water

Heat a small nonstick pan with 2 teaspoons of olive oil over medium-high heat. Once the oil is heated, add the shallots and cook until softened, about 5 minutes. Transfer to a medium bowl and allow to cool.

Combine the remaining ingredients for the nikudango in the bowl, except for the canola oil. Stir together until just combined. Split into 16 equally sized, round nikudango. Cover and allow the nikudango to rest in the refrigerator for at least 20 minutes.

Heat a large pan with canola oil over medium-high heat. Add the nikudango and brown each side until cooked through, about 3 to 5 minutes per side. Transfer to a plate.

Combine all the ingredients for the sauce in a medium saucepan. Heat over medium-high heat until the sauce is heated through. Add the nikudango and simmer for 5 minutes.

THEROS

〜◎◎◎◎◎◎◎◎◎◎◎〜

You might know me as Xenagos, the God of Revels. Well, former God of Revels. I was cheated out of my rightful place in the pantheon. I was even denied entry into the Underworld after my death, but who wants to skulk about in the dark with Erebos and Athreos anyhow? I only ever wanted to bring joy to all with my food-filled revelry. Some say that Meletis philosophers are stuffy, but I know better. When they stop debating and head to the eatery, they know how to celebrate. Everyone in Akros wakes up early to train in the hot sun, but there are secret taverns where hoplites are happy to break the rules in the city-state that has a moratorium on fun.

Technically, I'm dead—but that doesn't stop me from planning a delicious return. According to the philosophers, no god ever truly dies on Theros as long as someone still believes in them. There must be a satyr who wants me back, bless his bleating heart. Or maybe I'm just someone's nightmare come to life (looking at you, Ashiok!). Most likely, I'm an Eidolon, a chorus of one, destined to give commentary on the gods, heroes, and monsters of my homeland from the great beyond. Whatever I am, I believe it's time to create a new pantheon. Say goodbye to the old gods of Theros! We'll kick old Kruphix over the edge of the horizon and send Thassa to the belly of Arixmethes. My pantheon will be stuffed with planeswalkers who, like me, have a special affinity for this sun-kissed plane. I've planned perfect dishes, so that they won't be able to refuse. Watch out, Theros: There's going to be a new divine order, and it all starts with this ambrosial feast!

Xenagos's Divine Dip

Difficulty: ■☐☐☐ • **Prep Time:** 20 minutes • **Yield:** 6 servings • **Dietary Notes:** Vegetarian, Gluten-Free

To keep godly status on Theros, you must keep your name on people's lips. At your next festival, whip up this dip in honor of me, God of Revels.

2 serrano peppers

1 jalapeno pepper

2 garlic cloves

1 teaspoon red pepper flakes

3 tablespoons olive oil,
additional for serving

2 teaspoons red wine vinegar

12 ounces feta cheese,
additional for serving

6 ounces Greek yogurt

Place the serrano, jalapeno, and garlic in a food processor. Pulse until finely chopped.

Note: *If you want to reduce the heat of this dish, remove and discard the seeds and capsaicin glands.*

Add the remaining ingredients and mix together until well combined. Transfer to a serving dish. Top with a drizzle of olive oil and extra crumbled feta cheese.

ELSPETH'S "FINALLY FOUND HOME" STEW

Difficulty: ■■■□□ • **Prep Time:** 30 minutes • **Cook Time:** 45 minutes
Yield: 4 serving • **Dietary Notes:** Dairy-Free, Gluten-Free

It's probably a surprise to hear that I don't mind Elspeth, since she stabbed me and ruined all my hopes and dreams. But see, I've forgiven her. She broke out of the Underworld and sought vengeance upon the God of the Sun himself— which makes her my hero. And now he's locked away in a dark prison, and Elspeth is strutting around the Multiverse again. No matter where she wanders, Theros is her true home. After so much running, it's time she settled down here as the new, improved god of the sun. This first dish is in honor of Elspeth, our catch of the day.

1 whole red snapper, guts discarded

4 cups vegetable broth

3 cups water

olive oil

3 shallots, chopped

4 garlic cloves, chopped

2 carrots, chopped

2 celery stalks, chopped

3 Yukon Gold potatoes, peeled and chopped

zest and juice of 2 lemons

kosher salt

ground black pepper

Place the whole snapper, vegetable broth, and water in a large pot. Heat over medium-high heat and bring to a boil. Reduce the heat to low and simmer for 30 minutes. Strain and transfer the broth to a large bowl.

Remove the fish meat and discard the skin and bones. Set the meat aside for later.

In a medium, clean pot, add olive oil and heat over medium-high heat. Add the shallot and garlic and cook until softened, about 5 minutes. Add the carrots and celery, cooking until softened, another 5 minutes. Add the broth and potatoes.

Bring to a boil and then reduce the heat to medium-low. Simmer until the potatoes have cooked through, about 8 to 10 minutes.

Note: *Make sure to not overcook the potatoes. You do not want them to become mushy.*

Add the lemon zest and juice. Stir well and season with salt and pepper.

Add the fish meat and heat back up before serving. This soup should be enjoyed the day it is made.

NIKO'S "PERFECT TARGET" LAMB

Difficulty: ■■□□□ • **Prep Time:** 30 minutes • **Cook Time:** 4 ½ minutes

Yield: 6 servings • **Dietary Notes:** Gluten-Free

Let me raise a glass to Niko Aris, who is already a god in my eyes. To be a javelin-thrower on Theros is about as close to divine as a mortal could get, and Niko was the best of the best. But they didn't want to rest on their laurels. They defied their destiny and bravely took control of their own fate. I admire that, especially since things didn't quite go my way when I tried. Here's to Niko, who slaughtered the lamb of expectations and became a hero. May this dish celebrate their journey and bring them home again.

12 garlic cloves

3 shallots

3 rosemary sprigs

4 oregano sprigs

3 lbs lamb shoulder,
    cut into large chunks

1 lb Yukon Gold potatoes,
    cut in half

2 teaspoons kosher salt

1 teaspoon ground black pepper

⅓ cup olive oil

1 teaspoon ground cinnamon

1 teaspoon ground cumin

1 tablespoon honey

zest and juice of 1 lemon

8 ounces feta, cut into large chunks

butcher twine

Preheat oven to 350°F. Place 4 garlic cloves, shallots, leaves of 2 rosemary sprigs, and leaves of 3 oregano sprigs in a food processor. Pulse until the shallots and garlic are chopped. Add salt, pepper, olive oil, cinnamon, cumin, honey, and lemon juice. Pulse until it becomes a smooth sauce and set aside.

Prepare a large deep baking dish by lining it with aluminum foil. Place two sheets of parchment paper inside, enough to wrap the contents we will be adding. Place the lamb shoulder, potatoes, and remaining garlic cloves on the parchment paper. Add the sauce and massage into the lamb.

Wrap this with the parchment paper and tie closed with kitchen twine. Wrap the baking dish with aluminum foil to seal everything in. Place in the oven and bake for 4 hours, or until the lamb is tender.

Once tender, remove the top layer of aluminum foil and unwrap the parchment paper. Increase the oven to 425°F. Add the feta and bake for another 15 to 20 minutes to heat the feta and crisp up the lamb slightly.

KYTHEON'S LAMENT

Difficulty: ■■■□□ • **Prep Time:** 45 minutes • **Cook Time:** 1 ½ hours • **Yield:** 6 servings • **Dietary Notes:** N/A

Whether you know him as Gideon or Kytheon, he was an epic war hero and backbone of the Gatewatch. From Akros street kid to savior of the Multiverse, his story is one for the ages. They say Gideon died on Ravnica, and that his soul is wandering, looking for rest. Well, lament no longer, son of Theros! Come back to me, and before your nickname-slinging peers, I will crown you God Beefslab.

Eggplant

3 eggplants

olive oil

kosher salt

ground black pepper

Bechamel Sauce

¼ cup unsalted butter

¼ cup all-purpose flour

1 ⅔ cups milk

½ teaspoon nutmeg

¼ cup parmesan

ground black pepper

kosher salt

Filling

olive oil

1 onion, chopped

3 garlic cloves, chopped

½ teaspoon ground cinnamon

2 teaspoons dried oregano

1 teaspoon kosher salt

½ teaspoon ground black pepper

1 lb ground beef

½ cup red wine

15 ounces tomatoes, chopped

1 ounce mint, chopped

2 ounces parsley, chopped

Eggplant

Preheat oven to 400°F. Prepare a baking sheet with parchment paper. Cut the eggplants in half lengthwise and score the interiors. Rub all parts of the eggplant with olive oil. Season generously with salt and pepper.

Place on the prepared baking sheet, skin side up. Roast for 30 minutes. Turn to skin side down and set aside until the filling is ready.

Bechamel Sauce

Heat a saucepan over medium-high heat. Add the butter and heat until melted. Add the flour and cook until thick and it smells like baking bread. Slowly add the milk while constantly stirring the mixture. The sauce should remain decently thick and creamy. Add the nutmeg and parmesan and mix in well. Season the sauce with salt and pepper to your liking. Set aside until assembly.

Filling

Heat a medium nonstick pan over medium-high heat. Add 1 tablespoon of olive oil and the onions. Cook until softened and translucent, about 8 minutes. Add the garlic and cook until fragrant, about 2 minutes.

Add the cinnamon, oregano, salt, and pepper. Mix until well coated. Add the beef and cook until it has all browned.

Add the red wine. Scrape the bottom of the pan to release any bits that may have stuck to the bottom. Cook until the wine reduces by three-quarters. Add the chopped tomatoes and mix together well. Cook until most of the liquid has reduced, about 15 minutes.

Remove from the heat and mix in the mint and parsley.

Place the filling on each of the eggplant halves. Top with a generous amount of bechamel. Bake in the oven for 10 minutes at 400°F. Turn on the broiler and cook until the bechamel browns slightly, about 2 to 3 minutes.

Ajani's "Lost Kitty" Treats

Difficulty: ■■■□ • **Prep Time:** 45 minutes • **Inactive Time:** 4 hours • **Cook Time:** 1 ½ hours
Yield: 33 treats • **Dietary Notes:** Vegetarian

Ajani is a natural fit for my pantheon because he already hates the current gods of Theros. He blames them for what happened to Elspeth, and rightly so. Kind-hearted Ajani is the pal you want to have around in good times and in bad. He always sees the best in people, even those who don't deserve it. I've heard he's had a rough time of it lately, a proper dark night of the soul as it were. Ajani's always been the shoulder to cry on, but who will help him in his time of need? We will! We'll call that lost kitty home to Theros with this dessert that's as sweet as him.

Filling

¾ cup pistachios

⅓ cup almonds

¾ cup walnuts

1 teaspoon cinnamon

½ teaspoon cloves

¼ cup sugar

pinch of kosher salt

Assembly

¾ cup unsalted butter, melted

Twenty-two 9-by-14-inch phyllo dough sheets, defrosted

2 long skewers

Syrup

1 cup water

1 cup sugar

½ cup honey

2 lemon peels

1 cinnamon stick

2 tablespoons lemon juice

Preheat oven to 350°F. Place the pistachios, almonds, walnuts, cinnamon, cloves, and sugar in a food processor. Pulse until the nuts are chopped. Set aside.

Prepare a 9-by-13-inch deep pan by rubbing it with butter. Take a sheet of phyllo dough and brush with butter. Sprinkle about 1 tablespoon of the filling mixture over the phyllo.

Note: *You don't want to overfill the pan. Make sure there is a thin layer of nuts spread but not so many that they will be hard to work with.*

Take another phyllo sheet and lay it on top. Sprinkle another tablespoon of the filling on top. Place the 2 skewers in the center of the phyllo. This will make it easier to roll up. Fold the phyllo over the skewers. Roll the phyllo up, but not too tightly. Once rolled, press the edges of the tube toward the center, to create a ripple effect on the tube. Remove the skewers and place in the prepared pan.

Repeat with the remaining phyllo until you have 11 rolls. Cut each of the rolls into three portions. If you have any butter remaining, pour it over the top.

Place in the oven and bake for 1 hour, until the phyllo dough has turned golden brown.

While they are baking, prepare the syrup. Combine water, sugar, honey, lemon peels, cinnamon stick, and lemon juice in a saucepan over medium-high heat. Whisk until the sugar has dissolved, then bring to a boil. Reduce the heat and simmer for 20 minutes. Remove from the heat and set aside.

Once the pastries have finished baking, immediately pour all of the syrup over them. Allow to set for 4 hours at room temperature. Transfer to an airtight container and store at room temperature for up to 2 weeks.

Ashiok's Nightmare Muse

Difficulty: ■□□□□ • **Prep Time:** 15 minutes • **Yield:** 1 drink • **Dietary Notes:** Vegan, Gluten-Free

Ashiok, a mysterious bringer of nightmares, will be a spine-chilling addition to my pantheon. Ashiok isn't from Theros, but they've done so much for this plane. They've toppled kings, made monsters weep, and inspired Elspeth to hotfoot it out of the Underworld. Ashiok would make a better Lord of the Underworld than that sulky Erebos anyway. With Ashiok as a god, your nightmares will join the revels, dancing out in the open for all to see. I can't wait to sit with Ashiok and clink glasses of smoky cocktails. They are truly an inspiration for my nightmare muse.

2 ounces ouzo

2 ounces bourbon

½ ounce cherry liqueur

2 ounces pomegranate juice

juice of ½ lime

2 dashes bitters

2 drops black food dye, optional

cherry wood for smoking

Fill a cocktail shaker with ice. Add ouzo, bourbon, cherry liqueur, pomegranate juice, lime juice, bitters, and black food dye. Shake thoroughly for 15 seconds. Pour through a mesh strainer into a glass, making sure to leave about 1 inch of space from the top of the glass to add the smoke.

Follow the instructions of your smoke gun (or similar device) to add the smoke to the drink. Serve immediately.

ZENDIKAR

Zendikar is a plane fit for adventurers. It's known for its unforgiving terrain, deadly fauna, and aggressive flora. There are priceless treasures hidden on every continent, and some truly should stay that way. Only the most intrepid adventurers will survive the journey and claim the rewards. Zendikar was once chosen to be a prison for the eldritch monsters known as the Eldrazi. It has been the site of conflicts that reverberated throughout the Multiverse. The local Zendikari know their home is a wild, turbulent place, and they like it that way.

Bruse Tarl was a nomad, caravan master, and veteran of the Eldrazi war. The head ox of his herd was a mangy-good-for-nothing-fleabag, but Bruse couldn't imagine life on the road without his trusty friend. In good times and in bad, Bruse knew to focus on putting one foot (or hoof) in front of the other. Their latest adventure had taken them to every continent on Zendikar. His head ox complained for the whole herd the entire time, particularly when they had to board a ship to sail to their destination. Bruse's philosophy was to swear at the bad, celebrate the good, and embrace that there were unfathomable things that would defy understanding. Like his ox.

Bruse had been running his own caravan for a while, and he felt tired, and his limbs felt heavy on this journey. He wasn't sure how many adventures he had left in him—but he also wasn't the type of man to mope around. He couldn't let the herd see him slumping, or they'd give him guff until the end of time. Committed to living his life fully (and avoiding embarrassment), he made sure to enjoy his favorite food from each continent they visited in case it was the last chance he got. At the end of the route was Sea Gate, the largest settlement in Zendikar. It was destroyed in the war with the Eldrazi, but it had been rebuilt and was a thriving community once again. Sea Gate was even the hub for the major expeditionary houses. Bruse mused to himself that many adventurers began—and ended—their journeys in the comforts found in Sea Gate's many taverns. And it was certainly time for him to join them.

ADVENTURER'S POUTINE

Difficulty: ■■■■□ • **Prep Time:** 1 hour • **Cook Time:** 6 hours • **Yield:** 6 - 8 servings • **Dietary Notes:** N/A

Bruse housed his herd in the most luxurious stable in town. Then he settled his tired bones in at Sachir's Tavern with a pint and stories to tell. Many of the patrons were familiar to him. Most were allies who had also fought the Eldrazi. Akiri and Kaza played cards in the back. Jori En waved at him from the bar, and he thought he glimpsed Commander Tazri's face among the crowd. His friends began gathering around him, and he blessed each of them with a good-natured insult. Savory, salty poutine was the last dish on his must-have list. He tied a napkin around his neck and was grateful to have something so delicious in the company of friends. As he enjoyed his meal, Bruse described his culinary adventures to his eager listeners.

Short Ribs and Broth

¼ cup all-purpose flour

2 teaspoons kosher salt

1 teaspoon ground black pepper

3 lbs beef short ribs

canola oil

1 carrot, roughly chopped

1 celery stalk, roughly chopped

1 onion, roughly chopped

6 cloves of garlic, roughly chopped

4 cups beef broth

1 cup water

4 thyme sprigs

1 rosemary sprig

2 bay leaves

3 dried shiitake mushrooms

1 tablespoon whole black peppercorns

Potato Wedges

¼ cup olive oil

1 teaspoon garlic powder

1 teaspoon onion powder

1 teaspoon oregano

½ teaspoon sage

pinch of cayenne pepper

½ teaspoon ground black pepper

1 teaspoon kosher salt

3 brown potatoes, cut into wedges or
   thick fries

Gravy Per Serving

3 tablespoons unsalted butter

¼ cup all-purpose flour

1 cup beef broth

kosher salt

ground black pepper

Assembly

⅙ of the potato wedges

⅓ cup cheese curds

shredded short ribs

1 scallion, diced

Short Ribs and Broth

Preheat oven to 250°F. Place the flour, salt, and pepper in a zip-top bag. Add the short ribs and shake until coated in flour.

Over medium-high heat, heat a dutch oven with 1 tablespoon of canola oil. Add the short ribs and brown all sides, about 3 to 5 minutes per side. Transfer onto a plate. If you need to do this in batches, add additional canola oil per batch.

Add 1 tablespoon of canola oil. Add the carrot, celery, onion, and garlic and cook until slightly softened, about 8 minutes.

Add the broth, water, and beef short ribs. Finally, add the thyme, rosemary, bay leaves, shiitake mushrooms, and whole peppercorns. Cover and place in the oven. Cook until the beef is tender and easily comes apart, about 5 to 6 hours.

Once the broth is ready, strain and set the broth aside. The broth can be stored in the refrigerator for up to 3 days.

Potato Wedges

Preheat the oven to 450°F. Combine the olive oil, garlic powder, onion powder, oregano, sage, cayenne pepper, pepper, and salt. Toss the potato wedges in the mixture.

Prepare a baking sheet with aluminum foil and nonstick spray. Transfer the seasoned potato wedges onto the sheet and place in the oven. Bake for 15 minutes. Toss and bake for another 15 minutes. Turn on the broiler and cook the wedges until they are crispy, about 4 to 5 minutes.

Gravy Per Serving

To prepare the gravy, place a pot over medium-high heat. Melt the butter in the pot. Once melted, whisk in the flour. Slowly add the broth while whisking. It is very important that you do this slowly while constantly whisking. This process will allow the gravy to become nice and thick. Bring to a boil and then reduce the heat. Simmer until the gravy has thickened. Season with salt and pepper.

Assembly

To serve, place a large portion of wedges in a bowl. Top with the cheese curds, shredded short ribs, and scallion. Finally, add the gravy on top.

STONEFORGER PAVLOVA

Difficulty: ■■■■■ • **Prep Time:** 45 minutes • **Inactive Time:** 2 hours • **Cook Time:** 1 ½ hours
Yield: 6 - 8 mini pavlovas • **Dietary Notes:** Vegetarian

Ondu was once home to a great kor empire. Its sprawling ruins were as unavoidable as discussions of its most famous scion: the planeswalker Nahiri. Nahiri witnessed the rise and fall of the empire and helped trap the Eldrazi on Zendikar. As a powerful lithomancer, she created the network of stone hedrons that shaped the Eldrazi's prison. The people of Ondu accept her, flaws and all, and consider her a beloved child of Zendikar. The Zulaport artisans named their signature stonefruit pavlova in her honor. Bruse always enjoyed one or three when passing through the coastal settlement. If he ever had the pleasure of meeting Nahiri, he would thank her for all she has done.

Peach Curd

2 peaches, peeled, seeds discarded, and sliced

3 egg yolks

½ cup sugar

2 tablespoons lemon juice

pinch of salt

¼ cup butter

Meringue

1 ¼ cups sugar

5 egg whites, room temperature

1 teaspoon cream of tartar

½ teaspoon vanilla extract

1 teaspoon cherry liqueur

1 ½ teaspoons cornstarch

Peach Curd

Place the peaches in a blender and blend until smooth. Pass through a fine mesh strainer to remove any large bits.

In a medium saucepan, whisk the egg yolks, sugar, and peach puree until the sugar dissolves and the mixture is smooth. Add the lemon juice and salt. Place over low heat and whisk until it becomes thick, about 10 minutes or until it reaches a temperature of 170°F.

Note: *To test if the curd is thick enough, dip a spoon in the mixture and run a finger across the back of it. If the trail holds, it is ready.*

Add the butter. Whisk until the butter is completely melted. Strain into an airtight container and allow to cool completely. Place in the refrigerator for at least 1 hour before serving. Can be refrigerated for up to 1 week.

Meringue

Preheat oven to 250°F. Place the sugar in a food processor. Blend for 1 minute to make superfine sugar. Prepare a baking sheet with parchment paper.

Place the egg whites in the bowl of a stand mixer with a whisk attachment (or large bowl with a hand mixer). Blend at medium-low speed until the eggs start to froth. Increase the speed to high and whisk until soft peaks form.

Slowly add the sugar, 1 tablespoon at a time. Introducing the sugar too quickly will cause the mixture to deflate. Blend until the egg whites have reached stiff peaks.

Add the cream of tartar, vanilla extract, and cherry liqueur. Whisk until just combined. Fold in the cornstarch until combined.

Continued on next page

Whipped Cream

1 ¼ cups heavy cream

3 tablespoons confectioners' sugar

1 teaspoon vanilla extract

Per Serving

cooked meringue round

whipped cream

peach slices

plumcot slice

cherries, pits removed and cut in half

blackberries

peach curd

Transfer to a piping bag with a large star tip. Prepare a baking sheet with parchment paper. Take the piping bag and create a 4-inch-wide disc for the base of the pavlova. On the edge of the disc, create a 3-inch-high wall of meringue. Repeat this until you've used all the meringue mixture. You should end up with at least 6 mini pavlovas.

Place in the oven and bake for 10 minutes. Reduce the heat to 225°F and bake for another 35 to 40 minutes, until the outside is dry and crisp. Turn off the heat and allow to cool in the oven for 2 hours before removing.

Whipped Cream

Place the ingredients for the whipped cream in a bowl and whisk until stiff peaks form. Place in the refrigerator to keep cool until you are ready to use it.

Per Serving

Fill the dip in the center of the meringue with whipped cream. Top with the fruit. Once the meringue is dressed up, serve immediately.

Optional: *Pour the peach curd directly over the pavlova or serve separately.*

"HEART AND SOUL" BABKA

Difficulty: ■■■□ • **Prep Time:** 1 hour • **Inactive Time:** 2 hours • **Cook Time:** 20 minutes

Yield: 6 buns • **Dietary Notes:** Vegetarian

A native of Bala Ged, Nissa Revane is a hero to those who know her story—including Bruse. Nissa can communicate with the Worldsoul of a plane and manipulate its leylines: the paths of mana that crisscross every world. Nissa used that connection to save Zendikar and other planes more than once. She's often in the company of the fiery Chandra, whose heart always compels her to help those in need. Nissa's kin baked beautiful, celebratory buns with two flavors to commemorate the perfect pair of Nissa and Chandra. Bruse counts himself as lucky to have been offered a copy of the delectable recipe, and luckier still to count these two as his friends.

Dough

¾ cup milk, warmed (100°F)

½ tablespoon active dry yeast

2 ½ cups all-purpose flour

1 cup whole wheat flour

5 tablespoons sugar

1 teaspoon kosher salt

2 eggs

1 teaspoon vanilla extract

½ teaspoon almond extract

6 tablespoons unsalted butter, room temperature

Chocolate Filling

3 tablespoons unsalted butter

4 ounces dark chocolate

3 tablespoons cocoa powder

¼ cup confectioners' sugar

1 teaspoon kosher salt

Peanut Butter Filling

½ cup creamy peanut butter

¼ cup confectioners' sugar

1 teaspoon kosher salt

Combine the milk and yeast. Allow the yeast to bloom, about 5 minutes. Combine the flours, sugar, and salt in a large bowl. Add the yeast mixture, eggs, vanilla extract, and almond extract. Mix until the dough just comes together.

While the dough begins to knead, add the butter 1 tablespoon at a time. Knead the dough for 5 minutes. If the dough is too sticky, add 1 tablespoon of flour at a time. If it is too dry, add 1 tablespoon of milk at a time. Transfer to an oiled bowl, cover, and let rest for 1 hour or until it has doubled in size.

Prepare the chocolate filling by placing the butter in a saucepan over medium heat. Allow the butter to melt. Once melted, add the chocolate, cocoa powder, confectioners' sugar, and salt. Mix together until the chocolate is melted. Remove from the heat and set aside.

Prepare the peanut butter filling by mixing together the peanut butter, confectioners' sugar, and salt until combined and smooth. Set aside.

Transfer the dough to a lightly floured countertop and punch down. Lightly knead for 1 minute. Divide into 6 equal portions and cover with a kitchen towel.

Take one of the portions and roll out into an 8-by-5-inch rectangle. Take a generous portion of the chocolate filling and spread it on the dough, leaving a ¼-inch border. Tightly roll the dough and pinch the seam to seal. Set aside.

Take another dough portion and roll out into an 8-by-5-inch rectangle. Take a generous portion of the peanut butter filling and spread it on the dough, leaving a ¼-inch border. Tightly roll the dough and pinch the seam to seal. Set aside.

Continued on next page

Syrup

1 tablespoon water

1 tablespoon amaretto

2 tablespoons sugar

Cut the two rolls in half lengthwise. Turn the cut ends upward. Take a chocolate half and a peanut butter half and lay them next to one another. Pinch one end together. Tightly braid the two pieces together and pinch the end of the braid together. Shape the braided log into a tight circle, and knot the two ends closed. Place on a baking sheet with parchment paper, leaving 3 inches in between each bun. Repeat this step with the other two halves.

Repeat with the remaining portions.

Once all the buns are set, cover the tray with a kitchen towel and allow to rest for 1 hour, or until risen.

Whisk together all the ingredients for the syrup. Place in a microwave and heat for 20 to 30 seconds. Whisk again and make sure the sugar is dissolved.

Preheat oven to 350°F. Brush each of the buns with the syrup. Place in the oven and bake for 20 minutes, or until golden brown.

Battered Leylines

Difficulty: ■■■□□ • **Prep Time:** 30 minutes • **Cook Time:** 4 minutes per batch
Yield: 4 servings • **Dietary Notes:** Vegetarian

Akoum is geologically unstable, but strange plant life manages to thrive in the volcanic fumes. It's difficult to make a reliable map of Akoum because of the shifting terrain. Bruse couldn't be held back by such a minor inconvenience. He grew up here, running over the moving land and breathing the fumes; he has never gotten lost. Even though the land shifts regularly, the leylines remain constant. Like Nissa, the Akoum shamans can harness the power of the leylines to fight their enemies. Bruse's chest swelled with pride as he recalled the epic stand that he, the other Goma Fada nomads, and the shamans made against the Eldrazi. Battered, but not broken, they prevailed. When the fighting was done, all anyone craved (Bruse especially) were crunchy, salty, fried delicacies.

Wasabi Dipping Sauce

1 tablespoon wasabi

¼ cup mayo

¼ cup sour cream

1 tablespoon yuzu juice

Tempura

peanut oil

¾ cup cake flour

1 teaspoon baking soda

2 tablespoons potato starch

1 egg

1 cup carbonated water, ice-cold

2 ice cubes

1 lb asparagus

Prepare the wasabi dipping sauce by whisking together all of the ingredients. Place in an airtight container. Can be stored in the refrigerator for up to 2 weeks.

Fill a deep pot with 1 ½ inches of peanut oil and heat over medium heat to 350°F. Combine the cake flour, baking soda, potato starch, egg, and carbonated water in a medium bowl. Mix until the batter just comes together. It should be runny and ribbony when it pours from a spoon. Add the ice cubes to keep this mixture chilled.

Once the oil has heated up, dip the asparagus in the batter, then place in the oil. Fry for 1 minute, flip, and fry for another minute, or until golden brown. Transfer to a plate lined with paper towels to drain. Repeat until all the asparagus is cooked.

Note: *Do not overcrowd the pan as you are frying. If you put too many pieces in, the temperature will drop drastically and cook the asparagus poorly.*

"Ornery Brute" Curry

Difficulty: ■■■☐☐ • **Prep Time:** 45 minutes • **Cook Time:** 30 minutes
Yield: 4 - 6 servings • **Dietary Notes:** Vegan

Murasa is a towering plateau that rises from the sea. The Kazuul Road, which traverses the Cliffs of Kazuul, is the only way to reach the interior of the continent. It winds up hairpin curves with sheer drops that churn the stomachs of even the most seasoned caravanners. The Kazuul Road was where Bruse's head ox earned his first epithet: the Ornery Brute. The creature hated the route, and only the promise of his favorite curry would convince him to make the trek. Once they are safe at the top, Bruse, his Ornery Brute, and the rest of the herd always enjoy a hearty portion together as they gaze out at the sea far below.

Green Curry Paste

1 teaspoon black peppercorns

½ teaspoon Sichuan peppercorns

½ teaspoon coriander seeds

½ teaspoon cumin seeds

1 bunch cilantro

8 garlic cloves, smashed

1 shallot, cut in half

5 scallions, cut in half

2 Thai green chilies, stems removed

1 serrano pepper, stem removed

One 1-inch piece of ginger,
   peeled and sliced

2 lemongrass stalks, smashed

2 teaspoons kosher salt

1 teaspoon sugar

zest and juice of 1 lime

2 teaspoons canola oil

Curry

canola oil

16 ounces firm tofu, cut into
   bite-sized pieces

1 carrot, shredded and sliced

8 shiitake mushrooms, sliced

8 ounces sugar snap peas

1 red bell pepper, sliced

4 baby bok choy

15 ounces coconut milk

2 cups vegetable broth

juice of 2 limes

kosher salt

limes

cilantro

Green Curry Paste

Place the peppercorns, coriander seeds, and cumin seeds in a small pan. Heat over medium-high heat and toast until fragrant, about 3 to 5 minutes. Transfer to a spice grinder (or mortar and pestle) and grind until finely ground.

In a food processor, combine the ground spices and remaining ingredients for the curry paste and pulse until the mixture resembles a thick salsa. If the paste is too thick, add a few tablespoons of water. Store in the refrigerator until you are ready to use. Can be stored in the refrigerator for up to 1 week.

Curry

Place the tofu between two plates and top with a heavy object. Allow this to rest for 5 minutes in order to remove excess liquid.

Heat a pan with 1 teaspoon of canola oil over medium-high heat. Add the tofu and cook until all sides have slightly browned, about 2 to 3 minutes per side. Transfer to a plate.

Add another 2 teaspoons of oil in the pan along with all of the vegetables. Cook until the vegetables have softened lightly, about 8 minutes. Add the tofu and mix together.

Add the green curry paste, coconut milk, and vegetable broth. Bring to a boil. Reduce the heat and simmer for 10 minutes. Add the lime juice. Season with salt. Serve with a bowl of rice or rice noodles, lime quarters, and freshly chopped cilantro.

HEDRON CRAB CAKE BENEDICT

Difficulty: ■■■□ • **Prep Time:** 50 minutes • **Cook Time:** 20 minutes • **Yield:** 4 servings • **Dietary Notes:** N/A

Guul Draz had great weather, but Bruse generally avoided it for other reasons—including but not limited to bloodthirsty vampires, bloodsucking mosquitos, and soul-sucking swamps. As his pocketbook often reminded him, Guul Draz was home to the Free City of Nimana where people were eager to trade, so Bruse occasionally made an exception. What his heart truly desired was to visit the fish markets where they sold the most exquisite dish: hedron crab. Normal crab was delicious, but crabs who lived near the stone hedrons had a mind-blowing taste that was completely unique. Many hedrons had been destroyed in recent upheavals, but the important thing was that there was still an abundance of them in the swamps, which were teeming with crabs.

Hedron Crab Cake

3 tablespoons mayo

2 tablespoons Dijon mustard

½ teaspoon worcestershire sauce

zest and juice of 1 lemon

1 teaspoon celery salt

1 teaspoon ground black pepper

1 teaspoon ground mustard

½ teaspoon ground ginger

½ teaspoon ground fennel

½ teaspoon allspice

½ lb crab meat

1 egg

1 scallion, diced

¾ cup panko

canola oil

Hollandaise

4 egg yolks

1 tablespoon water

pinch of kosher salt

¼ teaspoon cayenne pepper

½ teaspoon paprika

juice of ½ lemon

8 tablespoons unsalted butter, melted

Hedron Crab Cake

Combine the mayo, Dijon mustard, worcestershire sauce, lemon zest and juice, and all the spices in a large bowl. Add the crab meat, egg, scallions, and panko and mix together well. Split into 4 portions. Form the mixture into hedron-like (diamond) shapes. They should be compact but not too tight.

Heat a pan with 1 tablespoon of canola oil over medium-high. Place the crab cakes in the pan and cook until golden brown on both sides, about 4 to 5 minutes per side.

Hollandaise

Fill a pot with 1 inch of water and place over medium-high heat. Select a bowl that fits the pot rim without touching the water. In the bowl, combine the egg yolks, water, salt, cayenne pepper, and paprika. Whisk together for 2 minutes.

When the pot of water comes to a low boil, place the bowl above it. Reduce the heat to medium-low. Begin to whisk continuously. Occasionally remove the bowl from the heat while maintaining your whisking to keep the temperature from rising too quickly. If the yolks cook too quickly, they will scramble.

Slowly add the melted butter, at most 1 tablespoon at a time. If you add the butter too quickly, the sauce will break, and you will have to start again. A broken sauce means the butter and the egg yolks have separated.

Once all the butter has been added, whisk in the lemon juice. Cover, set aside, and keep warm. The sauce will thicken as it cools. If the sauce thickens too much, place back on the steaming water before serving and add water to loosen the sauce up.

Continued on next page

Poached Eggs

2 teaspoons vinegar

4 eggs, each opened in a small bowl

pinch of salt

Per Serving

1 avocado, sliced

4 pieces European-style bacon, cooked

Poached Eggs

In a pan, place 1 inch of water and bring it to a boil. Add 2 teaspoons of vinegar and a pinch of salt. Carefully crack the eggs and slowly pour them into the water. Cook them for 4 ½ minutes. Remove the eggs and place on a paper towel to dry.

Assembly

To assemble, place a hedron crab cake on a plate. Place ¼ of the avocado on top of the crab cake. Top with a piece of bacon and then the poached egg. Drizzle with hollandaise. Serve immediately.

EMRAKRULLER

Difficulty: ■■■□ • **Prep Time:** 45 minutes • **Cook Time:** 1 hour • **Yield:** 20 - 22 krullers • **Dietary Notes:** Vegetarian

Before the Eldrazi, Sejiri was a landscape of windswept taiga with snowy peaks on the horizon. Bruse only visited a few times before the war. Despite his preference for the warmer climes, he was in awe of its stark beauty and hardy creatures like the snow gnarlids and the yetis. The Eldrazi devastated Sejiri, but the land and its wildlife rebounded. While Ulamog and Kozilek were defeated, the people of Sejiri make this twisted fare in remembrance of Emrakul, the one titan that got away. As they waited for their ship to take them to Sea Gate, Bruse shared a bite with extra frosting with his head ox one last time.

Dough

¼ cup + 2 tablespoons milk

2 tablespoons heavy cream

½ cup water

½ cup unsalted butter

1 tablespoon sugar

1 teaspoon vanilla paste

1 teaspoon kosher salt

1 cup all-purpose flour

4 eggs

peanut oil for frying

Raspberry Glaze

6 ounces raspberries

1 tablespoon lemon juice

1 tablespoon sugar

3 tablespoons unsalted butter

2 ounces white chocolate

pinch of kosher salt

2 cups confectioners' sugar

1 tablespoon heavy cream

1 teaspoon vanilla paste

Dough

Prepare 24 pieces of 5-by-5-inch pieces of parchment paper. Set aside.

Whisk together the milk, heavy cream, water, butter, sugar, vanilla paste, and salt in a saucepan over medium-high heat. Bring to a gentle boil and mix until the butter has melted and sugar has dissolved. Add the flour and mix until it comes together. Remove from the heat. Keep mixing until smooth.

Fill a deep pot with 2 inches of peanut oil and heat over medium heat to 360°F.

Transfer the batter to a stand mixer with a paddle attachment. Mix until it is cool to touch. Once cooled, add the eggs one at a time. Mix until completely combined. Transfer to a piping bag with a large star tip. Pipe a 3-inch donut on a single piece of parchment paper. Repeat this until all of the dough is used.

Once the oil is heated, carefully place 4 to 5 krullers in the oil, parchment paper on top, and cook for 2 to 3 minutes. Remove the parchment paper from the oil. Flip the kruller, then cook for another minute, or until both sides are golden brown. Remove from the oil and place them onto a plate covered with a paper towel. Repeat these steps with the remaining krullers.

Raspberry Glaze

Puree the raspberries and pass through a mesh strainer to remove the seeds. Combine the raspberry puree, lemon juice, and sugar in a saucepan over medium-high heat.

Whisk together until the sugar dissolves. Allow to simmer for 3 minutes. Remove from the heat and add the butter, white chocolate, and salt. Mix until well combined.

Add the confectioners' sugar and whisk together. Mix in the heavy cream and vanilla paste. If you would like the frosting to be a bit more pink, add a few drops of pink food dye. Dip each of the krullers in the glaze before serving.

KALADESH

Chandra Nalaar was born on Kaladesh, and is proud to call the vibrant, innovative plane her home. She is often called away to other planes for death-defying battles, but she loves returning to the capital city, Ghirapur. The city has all the ingredients that make Chandra happy: an energetic vibe, a dash of creativity, and an extra helping of optimism. Chandra is a positive person who watches out for the underdogs and has a profound hope for the future. Chandra *feels* a lot. It makes her compassionate, but it can be overwhelming. The food of Kaladesh brings back poignant memories for Chandra. A passing whiff of bread baking takes her back to childhood dinners. The fragrance of saffron conjures images of eating street food with friends. The warm aroma of roasting chicken reminds her of her father's cooking, which helped her cope when the world crashed down around her. She could write it all down, all of her favorite foods from Kaladesh, and keep them and the precious moments close when she was far from Kaladesh. She would! And so, she did.

JUMPSTART ENERGY BOWLS

Difficulty: ■■☐☐☐ • **Prep Time:** 30 minutes • **Cook Time:** 25 minutes • **Inactive Time:** 45 minutes
Yield: 1 bowl • **Dietary Notes:** Vegetarian

Aether is an energy that flows through the whole Multiverse, but it manifests on Kaladesh in a unique way. It swirls in the atmosphere in beautiful arcing tendrils. More than just pretty to look at, the aether is harnessed to power Kaladesh's many wondrous inventions. The denizens also seem to brim with energy, and that is reflected in their architecture and cuisine. Even on her most chaotic days, Chandra took the time to refuel in the morning (even if she forgot to go to sleep the night before). She swore that eating something sweet and vibrant assured a successful start to the day.

Granola

3 cups old-fashioned rolled oats

1 cup walnuts, chopped

½ cup almonds, chopped

½ cup cashews, chopped

½ cup unsalted butter

½ cup honey

3 tablespoons brown sugar

1 teaspoon ground cinnamon

1 teaspoon ground ginger

¾ teaspoon ground cardamom

½ teaspoon ground allspice

¼ teaspoon ground cloves

1 teaspoon kosher salt

⅔ cup dried cherries

⅓ cup golden raisins

Tea Yogurt

½ cup plain yogurt

1 teaspoon Assam tea

⅛ teaspoon ground cinnamon

⅛ teaspoon ground cardamom

⅛ teaspoon ground ginger

⅛ teaspoon ground cloves

1 ½ ounces acai

¾ cup frozen mixed berries

½ cup frozen blackberries

Per Serving

¾ cup granola

tea yogurt

banana, sliced

fresh raspberries

fresh blackberries

Granola

Preheat oven to 350°F. Prepare a baking sheet with a sheet of parchment paper. Combine the rolled oats, walnuts, almonds, and cashews in a large bowl. Set aside.

Combine the butter, honey, brown sugar, cinnamon, ginger, cardamom, allspice, cloves, and salt in a saucepan. Place over medium heat and mix together until the butter has melted and the sugar has dissolved. Carefully pour this into the large bowl with the oat mixture. Mix together until well combined.

Transfer to the baking sheet and spread into a thin layer. Place in the oven and bake for 10 minutes. Stir and bake for another 10 minutes. Stir once more and bake for 10 more minutes, or until golden brown. Remove from the oven and let cool for 45 minutes.

Once cooled, transfer to an airtight container. Mix in the dried cherries and raisins. This can be stored at room temperature in an airtight container for 10 days. This makes enough granola for about 10 portions.

Tea Yogurt

Place everything in a blender. Blend until smooth.

Per Serving

Place half of the granola at the bottom of a bowl. Add the tea yogurt. Top with the other half of the granola, banana slices, raspberries, and blackberries.

RENEGADE SPECIAL

Difficulty: ■■■□□ • **Prep Time:** 30 minutes • **Cook Time:** 30 minutes
Yield: 2 servings • **Dietary Notes:** Vegetarian, Gluten-Free

Pia Nalaar and Chandra thought they had lost each other. When Chandra found her mother again, she learned to treasure each moment they spent together. Pia usually cooks for Chandra when she's home. While Chandra doesn't have a lot of patience for the culinary arts, she took the time to perfect her mother's favorite dish. Every year on Pia's birthday, Chandra comes home to make her Renegade Special in honor of her mother's rebellious past. They share a drink, toast to the power of the people, and enjoy the moment together.

Green Chutney

1 bunch cilantro

3 tablespoons mint

2 serrano chilies, stems removed

3 garlic cloves

One 1-inch piece of ginger

1 teaspoon cumin seeds

½ teaspoon coriander seeds

1 teaspoon sugar

1 teaspoon kosher salt

1 teaspoon kala namak

juice of 1 lime

2 tablespoons water

Lemon Yogurt

¾ cup plain yogurt

juice of 1 lemon

Spiced Potatoes

1 teaspoon cumin seeds

½ teaspoon coriander seeds

½ teaspoon fennel seeds

½ teaspoon black peppercorns

1 black cardamom pod

1 green cardamom pod

3 russet potatoes, peeled and cubed

1 teaspoon amchur powder

½ teaspoon ginger powder

1 teaspoon kashmiri chili powder

1 teaspoon kosher salt

½ teaspoon kala namak

1 tablespoon fenugreek leaves

½ red onion, finely diced

1 serrano pepper, finely chopped

canola oil

Green Chutney

Place all of the ingredients in a blender and blend until smooth. If the mixture is too thick, add a small amount of water at a time to loosen it. Can be stored in an airtight container in the refrigerator for up to 1 week.

Lemon Yogurt

Whisk together the ingredients. Can be stored in an airtight container in the refrigerator for up to 1 week.

Spiced Potatoes

Place the cumin, coriander, fennel, peppercorns, and cardamom in a small pan. Heat over medium-high heat and toast until fragrant, about 3 to 5 minutes. Transfer to a spice grinder (or mortar and pestle) and grind until finely ground. Transfer to a bowl. Combine with amchur, ginger powder, kashmiri chili powder, salt, kala namak, and fenugreek leaves.

Bring a large pot of water to a boil. Add the potatoes and boil until tender, about 10 minutes. Drain, pat dry, and transfer to a plate. Allow to cool.

Place a large stainless-steel pan over medium-high heat with 2 tablespoons of canola oil. Allow to heat up and then add the potatoes. Fry until all sides are golden brown, 2 to 3 minutes per side. Transfer to a plate lined with paper towels.

Note: *Do not overcrowd the pan. You might have to do this in batches. Make sure to add more oil between each batch.*

Place the potatoes, red onion, and serrano pepper in a large bowl and toss to mix. Add the spice mixture and toss to coat.

To serve, split between 2 bowls and top with green chutney and lemon yogurt.

"Kiran's Memory"

Difficulty: ■■■□□ • **Prep Time:** 30 minutes • **Inactive Time:** 4 hours • **Cook Time:** 20 minutes
Yield: 10 chicken legs • **Dietary Notes:** Gluten-Free

Her father, Kiran Nalaar, died when Chandra was young. When she was a child, tandoori chicken was her favorite meal, and he made it for her often. She could still recall all the birthdays he cooked it for her. He made it to cheer her up when she was sad. He had the kindness in him to prepare it when they needed to have another discussion about "what Chandra did at school today." But it tasted the absolute best when he made it the night he gave her the regulator that helped control her wild pyromancy. Her father loved her no matter what, and "Kiran's Memory" is a part of him that she will treasure forever.

2 black cardamom pods

3 green cardamom pods

1 tablespoon cumin seeds

1 tablespoon coriander seeds

1 teaspoon black peppercorns

2 cloves

½ star anise

One 1-inch piece of cinnamon stick

1 bay leaf

1 tablespoon ground kashmiri
    chili pepper

2 teaspoons turmeric powder

pinch of nutmeg

1 tablespoon fenugreek leaves

2 teaspoons kosher salt

10 chicken legs

½ cup plain yogurt

juice and zest of 1 lemon

2 teaspoons ginger paste

1 teaspoon garlic paste

red food coloring, optional

Place the cardamom, cumin, coriander, peppercorns, cloves, star anise, and cinnamon in a small pan. Heat over medium-high heat and toast until fragrant, about 3 to 5 minutes. Transfer to a spice grinder (or mortar and pestle). Add the bay leaf and grind until finely ground. Transfer to a bowl and combine with kashmiri chili pepper, turmeric, nutmeg, fenugreek leaves, and salt.

Prepare the chicken legs by cutting deep slashes in the meat. Place in a large bowl. Add the spice mixture, yogurt, lemon juice and zest, ginger paste, garlic paste, and red food coloring. Mix very well until the chicken is completely covered.

Cover and allow the chicken to marinate for at least 4 hours, up to 6 hours.

Preheat the oven broiler to high. Prepare a baking tray with aluminum foil and then top with a wire rack. Place ¼ cup of water in the baking pan; this will help prevent too much smoke from appearing while cooking.

Transfer the chicken to the wire rack while making sure to remove any excess marinade on the pieces. Place the chicken directly below the broiler and allow to cook for 10 minutes.

Flip the chicken and cook for another 10 minutes. Check that the chicken is fully cooked, with an internal temperature of 165°F. If the chicken still needs more time, reduce the oven temperature to 350°F and bake until cooked through.

From Pachatupa to Ghirapur

Difficulty: ■■■□□ • **Prep Time:** 1 hour • **Cook Time:** 45 minutes • **Yield:** 8 servings • **Dietary Notes:** Vegetarian

Huatli is from Ixalan, and Saheeli is from Kaladesh. In recent years, the two planeswalkers have become some of Chandra's closest friends. Whenever she is in Ghirapur, they invite her over for burritos. Sometimes, they share stories from the war on Ravnica. But mostly they play a game that Huatli invented called Multiverse Trivia. Sample questions include: How many horns does an Ikorian Felidar have? Who created the Helvault? Where can you find a gnarlid? Saheeli usually wins. Chandra has only flipped the board once physically, but many more spiritually.

Ixalan Rice

2 tablespoons unsalted butter

½ onion, chopped

1 ½ cups basmati rice

2 teaspoons kosher salt

2 teaspoons cumin

1 tablespoon garlic powder

1 teaspoon onion powder

¼ cup tomato sauce

4 cups vegetable broth, warmed

pinch of saffron

1 bay leaf

Corn Slaw

½ cup mayo

½ cup sour cream

1 teaspoon kosher salt

2 teaspoons kashmiri chili powder

pinch of cayenne pepper

1 teaspoon paprika

1 teaspoon cumin

½ teaspoon garam masala

juice of 1 lime

2 tablespoons cilantro, finely chopped

3 scallions, green and white parts,
  finely chopped

½ red cabbage, thinly sliced

1 tablespoon unsalted butter

2 cups corn

1 jalapeno, seeds removed
  and finely chopped

Palak Paneer

18 ounces spinach

2 tablespoons ghee

4 garlic cloves, chopped

½ onion, chopped

One 1-inch piece of ginger, grated

1 serrano pepper, chopped

2 Roma tomatoes, diced

1 teaspoon cumin

2 teaspoons garam masala

3 tablespoons heavy cream

kosher salt

14 ounces paneer,
    cut into bite-sized pieces

Per Serving

large flour tortilla

refried beans

Ixalan Rice

Heat a saucepan with butter over medium heat. Melt the butter, add the onions, and cook until translucent. Add the rice and cook until slightly toasted, about 3 minutes.

Add the salt, cumin, garlic powder, and onion powder. Toss until everything is coated. Add the tomato sauce and cook for 2 minutes.

Add the vegetable broth, saffron, and bay leaf. Bring to a boil and then reduce the heat to low. Cover and cook until the rice has cooked, about 20 minutes.

Corn Slaw

Combine mayo, sour cream, salt, kashmiri chili, cayenne pepper, paprika, cumin, garam masala, lime juice, cilantro, scallions, and red cabbage in a medium bowl.

Heat a skillet with butter over medium-high heat. Add the corn and jalapeno. Cook and stir for 10 to 15 minutes, or until the corn has started to brown. Transfer to the bowl and mix well. Can be stored in an airtight container in the refrigerator for up to 5 days.

Palak Paneer

Bring a pot of salted water to a boil. Prepare a bowl with cold water and ice cubes, then set aside. Add the spinach to the boiling water and cook until wilted, about 30 seconds. Transfer immediately to the ice bath. Drain the spinach and lightly squeeze out the extra moisture. Place in a blender and blend until smooth. If it isn't blending easily, add a few tablespoons of water. Set aside.

Heat a medium pan over medium-high heat. Add the ghee and allow it to melt. Add the garlic, onions, ginger, and serrano peppers. Cook until the onion starts to turn golden, about 8 minutes. Add the diced tomatoes, cumin, and garam masala and cook for about 5 minutes.

Add the spinach and heavy cream. Mix together and taste. Add additional spices and salt to your liking. Toss in the paneer and coat in the sauce. Cook until the paneer is heated, about 3 to 5 minutes.

Per Serving

Heat up the tortillas and prepare to assemble. Take a tortilla and add a layer of refried beans. Top with the rice, slaw, and palak paneer and carefully wrap. Wrap the burrito in aluminum foil to serve.

"Welcome to the Fair" Samosa

Difficulty: ■■■□□ • **Prep Time:** 45 minutes • **Inactive Time:** 1 hour • **Cook Time:** 30 minutes
Yield: 12 samosas • **Dietary Notes:** Vegetarian

Chandra has sampled many street-fair samosas and charmed many sellers into sharing their recipes. This version is her absolute favorite.

Dough

2 cups all-purpose flour

1 teaspoon kosher salt

1 teaspoon ajwain seeds

5 tablespoons ghee, melted, then cooled

⅓ cup water

Filling

1 russet potato, peeled and chopped

2 teaspoons kosher salt

1 large onion, diced

1 tablespoon ginger paste

6 garlic cloves, minced

1 serrano pepper, diced

1 tablespoon cumin seeds

2 tablespoons coriander seeds

1 teaspoon ground turmeric

1 teaspoon ground kashmiri chili pepper

2 teaspoons garam masala

1 teaspoon amchur powder

1 teaspoon ground cinnamon

½ teaspoon ground cardamom

½ cup frozen peas

½ cup water

3 scallions, chopped

½ bunch cilantro, chopped

olive oil

peanut oil for frying

Dough

Combine the flour, salt, and ajwain seeds in a medium bowl. Mix in the ghee until it resembles coarse cornmeal. Add the water slowly and work until it forms a firm dough. If the dough is too sticky, add 1 tablespoon of flour at a time. If it is too dry, add 1 tablespoon of water at a time.

Form into a ball, place in the bowl, and cover with a kitchen towel. Let rest for 1 hour before filling.

Filling

Heat a pot with water (enough to just cover potatoes), potatoes, and 1 teaspoon salt over high heat. Bring to a boil and then reduce the heat and simmer for 15 to 20 minutes, or until the potatoes are tender. Drain and set aside.

Heat a large nonstick pan with 1 tablespoon of olive oil over medium-high heat. Add the onions and cook until softened, about 3 to 5 minutes. Add the ginger paste, garlic, and serrano pepper, and stir well. Add the cumin seeds, coriander seeds, turmeric, kashmiri chili, garam masala, amchur, cinnamon, cardamom, and remaining salt. Toss until the onion is coated in the spices.

Add the peas, toss together, and cook for 5 minutes. Add the potatoes and lightly mix together. Add the water and cover. Allow to cook until the water has evaporated, about 5 minutes.

Remove from the heat and mix in the scallions and cilantro. Lightly mash to bring everything together. Set aside and allow to cool completely.

Split the dough into 6 equal portions, keeping the dough you aren't working with covered.

Place one of the portions on a lightly floured surface. Roll out into a thin circle. Cut in half.

Take one of the halves and brush the cut edge with water. Take the corners of the cut edge and fold over one another and press together to form into a cone. Fill the cone with the filling. Lightly wet the edges and pinch together to seal the filling in. Repeat this step with the other half.

Repeat until all the dough has been used. Pour 1 inch of peanut oil in a deep pot and heat to 350°F.

Once the oil has been heated, place 3 of the samosas into the oil and fry for 3 minutes. Flip and fry for another 3 minutes, or until both sides are golden brown. Transfer to a plate with a paper towel. Repeat until all samosas have been fried.

LIFE OF THE PARTY

Difficulty: ■■■☐☐ • **Prep Time:** 40 minutes • **Inactive Time:** 4 hours • **Cook Time:** 30 minutes
Yield: 14 fried dough balls • **Dietary Notes:** Vegetarian

The aetherborn are beings created from the aether. They have short life spans, so they try to live their lives to the fullest, never wasting a second. Chandra counts Yahenni as one of her greatest teachers. They fought together to free Kaladesh from the iron fist of the Consulate. Yahenni was a joyful being and the life of any party. They were focused on existence, the here and now, and Chandra admired that. Sometimes, when darkness clouds her mind, Chandra seeks out the syrup-soaked fried dough balls served at Yahenni's final party. When she's done, she licks her fingers and hums Yahenni's favorite song. Then she thanks the Multiverse for all it has given and taken away.

Syrup

1 cup water

1 ½ cups sugar

2 green cardamom pods, crushed

2 pinches of saffron

2 lemon peels

Dough

1 ½ cups milk powder

¼ cup all-purpose flour

1 teaspoon sugar

1 teaspoon baking powder

¼ teaspoon ground cardamom

pinch of salt

3 tablespoons unsalted butter, room temperature

7 to 9 tablespoons milk

peanut oil for frying

Syrup

Combine water, sugar, and cardamom in a saucepan and place over medium-high heat. Whisk until the sugar has dissolved and it reaches a boil. Reduce the heat and simmer for 10 minutes.

Remove from the heat and add the saffron and lemon peels. Allow to rest for 45 minutes. Transfer into an airtight container and set aside.

Dough

Combine the milk powder, flour, sugar, baking powder, cardamom, and salt in a medium bowl. Cut the butter into small cubes and then add to the bowl. Combine with your hands until the mixture resembles coarse cornmeal.

Add the milk slowly and work everything together. If the dough is too dry, you can add additional milk. Knead until smooth.

Split into 14 equal portions and form into balls. Cover with a damp paper towel.

Pour 1 inch of peanut oil in a deep pot and heat to 275°F.

Add a few of the balls to the oil, making sure to not overcrowd the pot. Fry for 5 to 7 minutes, turning frequently, or until a nice golden brown. Drain well and transfer to a plate lined with paper towels to remove any excess oil. Repeat this step until all of the balls are fried.

Transfer the fried balls into the syrup and let set at room temperature for at least 4 hours before serving.

CHANDRA'S "FREE TO BE ME" LASSI

Difficulty: ■□□□□ • **Prep Time:** 15 minutes • **Yield:** 2 drinks • **Dietary Notes:** Vegetarian

When her emotions boil over, Chandra wishes she were more like Nissa, who is calm and cool as a serene lake. When she accidentally burns something down, she wishes she were more like Jace, who foresees the outcomes of impulsive actions. When she cries over someone's suffering, Chandra wishes she were more like Liliana, who controls her emotions with ease. And sometimes, when everything is overwhelming, she wishes she were more like Gids, who had been a bulwark against the evils of the world. Despite her optimism, she can beat herself up more than any bad guy. Above her intrusive thoughts, Chandra remembers drinking mango lassi with her cherished friends at a café. She started to say: "I wish I was more…" Everyone stood up—even Liliana—and put their arms around her. Nothing quieted her mind in the same way. That group hug told her she was enough just the way she was.

3 ataulfo mangoes

1 cup yogurt

½ cup water

¼ teaspoon ground cinnamon

½ teaspoon cayenne pepper, optional

Note: *The cayenne pepper will give this drink a kick. Feel free to adjust the amount to your liking or leave it out; both options are delicious.*

1 tablespoon honey

pinch of kosher salt

Place everything in a blender. Blend until smooth.
Split between 2 glasses.

IXALAN

Jace and Vraska have a turbulent history. During their association, there have been lies, betrayals, friendship, and profound respect. The pair originally met on Ravnica, where Vraska was an assassin for the Golgari. She plotted to kill Jace, the Living Guildpact of the plane. Her scheme failed, but Jace remained on Vraska's hit list. A chance encounter on a faraway plane would transform these enemies into allies. Despite their relationship's twists and turns, they can still set aside time to hoist a glass of rum, relax, and recount their star-crossed love and the tasty food they enjoyed on their journey.

DESERTED ISLE WRAP

Difficulty: ■■□□□ • **Prep Time:** 30 minutes • **Inactive Time:** 1 hour • **Cook Time:** 20 minutes

Yield: 4 servings • **Dietary Notes:** Dairy-Free, Gluten-Free

Known for its two continents and four factions, Ixalan was the setting for Jace and Vraska's epicurean adventure. As Jace recalls it, he had lost a battle with an evil dragon and was cast adrift into the Multiverse. Like metaphysical flotsam, he arrived on an unfamiliar plane. Marooned on an island in a vast ocean, Jace lost his memories and his shirt. But he at least kept his wits about him and devised a Plan A, a Plan B, and many more (until he ran out of letters). Jace attributes his survival of those first lonely days on Ixalan to clever thinking and an island dish born of improvisation.

2 teaspoons chili powder

1 teaspoon turmeric

1 teaspoon coriander

½ teaspoon cumin

½ teaspoon cinnamon

½ teaspoon kosher salt

½ teaspoon ground black pepper

2 tablespoons lime juice

¼ cup olive oil

4 (½ lb each) Chilean sea bass filets

4 (12-inch squares) banana leaves

Combine the chili powder, turmeric, coriander, cumin, cinnamon, salt, pepper, lime juice, and olive oil in a small bowl. Rub each of the sea bass filets with the sauce.

Take a banana leaf and place one of the filets in the center. Carefully wrap the fish until it is completely sealed within the banana leaf. Place on a baking sheet. Repeat with the remaining filets.

Place in the refrigerator to rest for 1 hour.

Preheat oven to 400°F. Remove the wrapped fish from the refrigerator and let sit at room temperature for 15 minutes.

Bake for 15 to 18 minutes, until the fish is cooked through, or the internal temperature reads about 145°F. Remove from the banana leaves and serve with Saucy Sailing Chimichurri (page 203).

SAUCY SAILING CHIMICHURRI

Difficulty: ■□□□□ • **Prep Time:** 15 minutes • **Yield:** 2 cups • **Dietary Notes:** Vegan, Gluten-Free

Just when all hope seemed lost, a pirate ship appeared on the horizon. The sight of Jace initially shocked Captain Vraska. But without his memories, Jace didn't recognize her—Vraska couldn't believe her luck. Poor, lost Jace was now at her mercy. She knew all about his powers even if he didn't. In exchange for helping her find the lost city of Orazca, she would spare his life. As they sailed toward the Sun Empire, Jace remembered his powers, and they used his illusions to raid other ships. Soon, they had established themselves as a pirate power couple. Love was in the crisp ocean air as the two embarked on a high-seas romance.

5 garlic cloves

1 bunch parsley, stems removed

1 bunch cilantro, stems removed

2 tablespoons fresh oregano

1 teaspoon kosher salt

¼ teaspoon ground black pepper

½ teaspoon pinch of sugar

1 teaspoon red pepper flakes

juice and zest of 1 lime

¼ cup apple cider vinegar

½ cup olive oil

Place the garlic, parsley, cilantro, oregano, salt, pepper, sugar, and red pepper flakes in a food processor. Pulse until finely chopped. Transfer to an airtight container.

Add the lime zest and juice, apple cider vinegar, and olive oil. Stir until well combined. Season with additional salt and pepper to your liking. Can be stored in an airtight container for 3 days.

SEADOG CEVICHE

Difficulty: ■■☐☐☐ • **Prep Time:** 30 minutes • **Inactive Time:** 2 hours • **Cook Time:** 2 - 3 minutes per batch
Yield: 4 servings • **Dietary Notes:** Dairy-Free, Gluten-Free

Jace and Vraska sailed under the flag of the Brazen Coalition, a group of loosely confederated pirates. The Coalition hates rules, loves freedom, and throws pirate parties that could last for days. High and Dry is a floating city and the hub for rummy revelries. The pubs of the city are famous for fresh seafood, which is often caught right in front of the customer. Jace and Vraska fondly remember stopping for a siesta in the notorious city and enjoying the freshest ceviche in the Seadog Inn. As the sun set over the crashing waves, Jace became more than a deckhand to Vraska. The two agreed to join forces to find the Golden City.

Ceviche

¼ red onion, thinly sliced

⅓ lb cod, cubed

3 large scallops, cubed

1 clove garlic, minced

½ jalapeno, seeded and minced

½ avocado, cubed

2 tablespoons cilantro, minced

3 ½ tablespoons lime juice

Plantain Chips

1 plantain, ripe

kosher salt

ground black pepper

peanut oil for frying

Ceviche

Place the red onion in a small bowl with ice and water. Let rest for 30 minutes. Drain and transfer to a medium bowl.

Add the cod, scallops, garlic, jalapeno, avocado, and cilantro. Lightly toss together. Add the lime juice and toss again. Cover and place in the refrigerator for 2 hours before serving.

Plantain Chips

Prepare the plantain by cutting it open, removing the skin, and slicing into very thin pieces. Season with salt and pepper.

Fill a frying pan with ½ inch of peanut oil and heat over medium heat. Once heated, carefully add the plantains and cook each side until golden, about 2 to 3 minutes per side.

Transfer to a paper towel on a plate to drain excess oil off. Don't leave them on the paper towel for too long or they can get stuck. Transfer to a clean plate. Serve warm.

THREE SUN CONCHAS

Difficulty: ■■■□ • **Prep Time:** 1 hour • **Inactive Time:** 3 hours • **Cook Time:** 20 - 25 minutes
Yield: 12 conchas • **Dietary Notes:** Vegetarian

The Sun Empire was the next stop of their whirlwind journey. Jace and Vraska less-than-legitimately secured invitations to the Shining Sun Celebration in Pachatupa, the capital city of the prosperous empire. The Threefold Sun embodies the three aspects that the Sun Empire admires most: order, growth, and passion. They incorporate this devotion in all areas of their daily lives, including food. As the warrior Huatli described the aspects in poetic detail, Vraska's and Jace's eyes met, and fireworks exploded in the sky. They shared an unforgettable moment sweeter than a plate of Three Sun Conchas.

Dough

¾ cup whole milk

1 tablespoon active dry yeast

4 ½ cups all-purpose flour

⅓ cup sugar

1 teaspoon kosher salt

1 teaspoon ground cinnamon

½ teaspoon ground cardamom

½ teaspoon grated nutmeg

3 eggs

1 teaspoon vanilla paste

6 tablespoons unsalted butter,
    room temperature

Cookie Topping

½ cup unsalted butter,
    room temperature

1 teaspoon vanilla extract

1 cup all-purpose flour

¾ cup powdered sugar

pinch of kosher salt

red food dye

green food dye

Combine the yeast and milk and let rest for 5 minutes, allowing the yeast to become active. Combine the flour, sugar, salt, cinnamon, cardamom, and nutmeg in the large bowl of a stand mixer. Add the yeasted milk, eggs, and vanilla paste to the bowl and mix until the dough just comes together.

While the dough begins to knead, add the butter 1 tablespoon at a time. Knead the dough for 5 minutes. If the dough is too sticky, add 1 tablespoon of flour at a time. If it is too dry, add 1 tablespoon of milk at a time.

Transfer to an oiled bowl, cover, and let rest for 2 hours, or until doubled in size.

About 30 minutes before the dough finishes its proofing, make the cookie topping. Place the butter and vanilla extract in a bowl and mix until the butter has softened completely. Add the flour, powdered sugar, and salt, and mix until combined.

Split the cookie topping into 3 equal portions. Take one of the portions and add a few drops of red food dye. Knead until it is completely dyed red. Repeat this with one of the other portions using the green food dye.

Split each of the 3 portions into 4 small balls; you should have 12 topping portions total. To make a multicolored cookie topping, cut a ball of each color into thirds. Carefully mold the thirds together to form balls with three colors. Cover the topping balls and set in the refrigerator until you are ready to use them. Try not to have these in the refrigerator for more than 30 minutes.

Once the dough has doubled, punch down and knead. Prepare 2 large baking sheets by placing parchment paper on them. Divide the dough into 12 portions. Shape into round balls and place on the prepared baking sheets with room to spread out.

To place the cookie topping, set one of the topping balls between two sheets of plastic wrap. Gently press down with a plate to shape into a flat disc, about the size of the dough rounds. Remove the top layer of plastic, then flip the topping onto one of the dough rounds. Lightly press down to adhere the topping to the dough. Remove the remaining plastic wrap.

Use a sharp knife to create slashes on the topping, similar to a seashell. Repeat with the remaining portions of cookie dough and topping.

Cover the baking sheets with a kitchen towel and allow to proof for 1 hour, or until doubled in size.

Preheat oven to 350°F. Remove the kitchen towels from the baking sheets. Place the baking sheets in the oven and bake the conchas for 20 to 25 minutes, or until the dough turns golden brown.

Braised "Dino" Ribs

Difficulty: ■■■□□ • **Prep Time:** 30 minutes • **Inactive Time:** 24 hours • **Cook Time:** 6 - 8 hours
Yield: 3 - 4 servings • **Dietary Notes:** Dairy-Free, Gluten-Free

The duo headed into the jungle. The Legion of Dusk, a fleet of vampires from across the Stormwreck Sea, had set a trap for them. Busy gazing into each other's eyes, Jace and Vraska were easily captured. The aristocratic vampires were also searching for the Golden City and tried to woo Jace and Vraska for information. They offered them a succulent dinner, which used local dinosaur meat instead of the customary Highland beef. When Jace and Vraska refused to talk, they found themselves on the menu. As the vampires encircled them, Vraska held them back with a concealed dagger. Jace sent them running with an illusion of a feathered giganotosaurus. But they weren't about to leave that dinner to go to waste.

5 lbs bone-in dino ribs, cut into sections

Note: *You want to cut the pieces to have one bone per section. Depending on the size of the ribs, you should end up with 3 to 4 large ribs.*

1 fennel bulb, quartered

2 celery ribs, roughly chopped

6 thyme sprigs

1 rosemary sprig

½ cup water

1 cup rice vinegar

1 tablespoon liquid smoke

¼ cup olive oil

2 teaspoons ground mustard

2 teaspoons paprika

2 teaspoons garlic powder

1 teaspoon onion powder

1 teaspoon ground fennel

Prepare a baking sheet with aluminum foil and top with a wire rack. Generously season the ribs with salt and pepper. Place on the wire rack and into the refrigerator uncovered. Allow to rest for at least 18 hours, up to 24 hours.

The next day, remove the ribs from the refrigerator and let rest at room temperature for 30 minutes. Preheat oven to 250°F. In a large, deep baking pan, add the fennel, celery, thyme, and rosemary. Pour in the water, rice vinegar, and liquid smoke.

Combine the olive oil, ground mustard, paprika, garlic powder, onion powder, and ground fennel in a small bowl. Brush each of the ribs with this mixture, making sure to thoroughly rub the mixture onto each of the pieces. Place the ribs in the baking pan on top of the vegetables, bone side down. Cover the pan in aluminum foil to seal everything in.

Place in the oven and bake for 6 to 8 hours, or until the meat reaches an internal temperature of 200°F. Remove and discard the aluminum foil. Turn on the broiler and crisp up the top of the meat until the fat turns a light golden brown, about 3 to 5 minutes.

Jade Toast

Difficulty: ■■□□□ • **Prep Time:** 1 hour • **Cook Time:** 30 minutes • **Yield:** 1 serving • **Dietary Notes:** Vegetarian

After escaping the Legion of Dusk, Jace and Vraska became lost in the jungle. Fortunately, the River Heralds, the jade-clad merfolk of Ixalan, came to their aid. The River Heralds were responsible for guarding the Golden City of Orazca, which was hidden by the jungle. They retained the old customs and cuisines of Orazca, and kindly shared the sustenance and knowledge Jace and Vraska needed to complete their quest. After finding the city, Jace and Vraska set sail for other adventures, but they never forgot their special summer of love in Ixalan.

Tomatillo Salsa

10 tomatillos, husks removed and cut in half

5 garlic cloves

1 jalapeno, cut in half and seeds removed

1 poblano, cut in half and seeds removed

½ red onion

1 bunch cilantro

5 scallions

2 limes, juiced

1 teaspoon kosher salt

1 teaspoon ground black pepper

Pico de Gallo

½ onion, chopped

1 jalapeno, chopped

2 large tomatoes, chopped

zest and juice of 2 limes

2 tablespoons cilantro

Per Serving

1 bolillo, sliced in half

8 ounces refried beans

4 ounces cheddar cheese

½ avocado

pico de gallo

2 eggs, cooked to your liking

tomatillo salsa

Tomatillo Salsa

Preheat oven broiler. Place the tomatillos, garlic, jalapeno, poblano, and onion on a baking sheet. Put the baking sheet under the broiler and cook until the tomatillos have charred slightly, about 10 minutes.

Remove from the oven and allow to cool. Transfer to a food processor. Add the cilantro, scallions, lime juice, salt, and pepper. Pulse in the food processor until smooth. Season with additional salt and pepper if needed. Can be stored in an airtight container in the refrigerator for up to 1 week.

Note: *The longer the salsa stays in the refrigerator, the more it will lose its green coloring.*

Pico de Gallo

Combine all of the ingredients together. Can be stored in an airtight container in the refrigerator for up to 1 week.

Per Serving

Top each of the bolillo halves with refried beans. Add the cheddar cheese on top. Place under a broiler and let cook until the cheese has melted, about 3 to 5 minutes.

Transfer to a plate. Top each half with avocado and pico de gallo. Place a cooked egg on top of each half. Finally, top with a generous portion of the tomatillo salsa.

Ingredients Glossary

AJWAIN SEEDS, also known as carom seeds, are a small, brown spice used in Indian cooking. These seeds have a strong, bitter flavor. Ajwain seeds can be stored in a cool pantry.

AMARETTO is a sweet almond liqueur. It has a slightly bitter, almond flavor to it. Amaretto can be substituted with almond extract. Note that almond extract is much more potent and should only be added at one-third the amount.

AMCHUR POWDER is a powder used in Indian cuisine. It is made from unripe mangoes that have been dried in the sun and then ground into a powder. It has a tangy and sour taste to it, similar to dehydrated mango. It can be stored in the pantry in an airtight container for about a year.

ARTICHOKE HEARTS are the tender center of the artichoke.

ASSAM BLACK TEA is a black tea from Assam, India. This is a heavy, full-bodied flavored tea. This can be substituted with another strong black tea.

ATAULFO MANGO is a variety of mango with a golden interior and exterior. It has a smoother texture and is slightly sweeter when compared to the Tommy Atkins variety.

BABY PORTOBELLO, also known as baby bella or cremini mushroom, is a dark brown, firm mushroom. These can be substituted for white mushrooms or full-sized portobello mushrooms, but make sure to cut them into smaller portions to fit the recipe's needs.

BAKED BEANS are a white bean dish that is then slow cooked in a tomato-based sauce. This can be found already prepared and canned.

BANANA LEAF is a leaf from the banana tree. For cooking, they are primarily used to wrap food similarly to aluminum foil. They add a very minor earthy flavor to the food that is wrapped within them.

BENI SHOGA is red pickled ginger.

BLACK GARLIC is garlic that has been heated and aged over weeks. During this time, the cloves will become tender and black.

BLACK RICE, also called purple rice, is a type of glutinous rice. When cooked with other rice, it will dye everything a deep, dark purple color.

BLUE CHEESE is a semi-soft cheese with a salty, pungent flavor that contains blue mold. There are many varieties of this cheese and any of them will work well when called for.

BOLILLOS are Central American bread rolls with a crusty exterior and light, fluffy interior.

BREAD FLOUR is a high-protein flour, typically containing 12% to 14% protein, meant to be used in yeasted breads. The higher protein in the flour helps create more gluten throughout the bread, making it more elastic and chewy.

BONITO FLAKES, also known as katsuobushi, are dried tuna shavings. They are one of the major components in dashi. Bonito flakes can be used to enhance the flavors of stocks and used as a garnish. Bonito flakes can be stored in a cool pantry.

BURDOCK is a root vegetable. When used as an ingredient for tea, it adds an earthy flavor.

BUTTERFLY PEA FLOWERS are dried flowers that grow in Southeast Asia. The flower is dehydrated and commonly used for tea. It is also used to dye things a bright blue color.

BUTTERMILK is a fermented milk. It is thicker than regular milk and has a tangy smell and flavor. When used in baking, it helps activate baking soda, leading to a much airier consistency. Buttermilk can be substituted for 1 cup of milk with 1 tablespoon of lemon juice.

BUZZ BUTTONS, also known as Sichuan buttons, are a bright yellow flower. Consuming these flowers will numb your mouth and increase salivation. After eating them (or just chewing), they will enhance the flavor of drinks or food you consume for a short period of time.

CARAWAY SEEDS are dried fruit of the caraway plant. They have a sharp, nutty, peppery flavor with a hint of licorice (anise). Caraway seeds can be substituted with fennel seeds.

CARDAMOM is a pod of seeds used in both savory and sweet dishes. They can be used as a whole pod or ground. The green variety has a very strong zesty, flowery, and earthy flavor suited for both savory and sweet dishes. Black cardamom has a smoky, menthol-like flavor great for savory dishes. The flavor of cardamom is pretty unique, but a combination of cinnamon, allspice, and nutmeg can serve as a substitute.

CHAMOMILE is a daisy-like flower known for its relaxing capabilities. When used for tea, the flower is typically dried and used just like any loose-leaf tea.

CHILEAN SEA BASS, also known as Patagonian toothfish, is an oily, flaky fish. It can be substituted for black cod or Atlantic cod.

CILANTRO, also known as coriander, includes the fresh leaves and stalks grown from coriander seeds. Cilantro has a citrusy, slightly peppery taste to it. Some individuals might find it to taste extremely soapy. Cilantro can be subbed for equal parts parsley.

CHICKEN FEET are an extremely gelatinous, collagen-heavy ingredient used in many styles of recipes. They are used in this book to help introduce a high level of gelatin to the paitan broth (page 129), giving it a creamy, thick texture. If you are unable to find them, they can be replaced with chicken wings.

CHEDDAR CHEESE is a mild-flavored hard cheese often covered in a hard wax to prevent a rind from forming on the outside. Substitutes for cheddar cheese include cantal, edam, and gouda.

CHEESE CURDS are a by-product of cheesemaking. They have a mild flavor similar to cheddar cheese. Fresh cheese curds have a texture that, when chewed on, will cause them to squeak. Substitutes can include fresh mozzarella balls or cheddar cheese.

CHESTNUT MUSHROOMS, also known as cinnamon cap mushrooms, are a bundle of dark golden-brown-colored mushrooms. Substitutes for these mushrooms include shiitake mushrooms and beech mushrooms.

CHOCOLATE BATONS, also known as chocolate baking sticks, are thin rectangle-shaped chocolates perfect for baking in pastries like chocolate croissants. They are typically made with less cocoa butter than other chocolate bars, which helps them keep their shape and not burn while baking.

CINNAMON is a spice derived from the inner bark of the *Cinnamomum* genus of evergreen. The bark is shaved and then dried to create the sticks. It is sold whole or ground. There are several varieties of cinnamon, but the ceylon variety is the variety that has been tested with all the recipes.

CONDENSED MILK is milk that has been gently heated, had 60% of the water removed from it, been mixed with sugar, and canned. This is an extremely thick, caramelized sweetened milk. It is typically found in cans that can be stored in a pantry for about a year. Once opened, it must be refrigerated and used within 2 weeks.

CONFECTIONERS' SUGAR, also known as powdered sugar, is granulated white sugar that has been ground into an extremely fine powder. This ingredient is typically used for thickening and sweetening frostings without giving them a grainy texture.

CORN SYRUP is a syrup sweetener made from sugars in corn. There are two main varieties of corn syrup: light, which is transparent with a mild flavor; and dark, which is much sweeter with a deeper, caramel-like color. The recipes in this book use the light variety.

CORIANDER SEEDS are dried, small, round seeds of the cilantro (also known as coriander) plant. These can be found as whole seeds or already ground. Coriander seeds can be replaced in equal parts with cumin seeds but will have a slightly different taste.

CRAB MEAT is the meat found in the shells of crabs. Soft-shell crab meat is what was used for recipes in this book, but any variety of crab meat can be used. Note that imitation crab meat is typically made from a variety of white fish.

CREAM CHEESE is a mild-flavored, soft, spreadable cheese. Substitutes for cream cheese include mascarpone, silken tofu, and neufchâtel.

DANMUJI is a yellow pickled radish used in Korean cuisine.

DARK RYE FLOUR is a type of rye flour typically consisting of more rye kernel when compared to a light rye flour. This variety has a much deeper rye flavor throughout the flour. Substitutes for dark rye flour include spelt flour, white flour, and whole wheat flour.

DASHI is a basic fish stock. It is made by combining kombu and bonito flakes with water. Dashi must be stored in the refrigerator once cooked and can be stored for up to 5 days.

"DINO RIBS" are full-length beef short ribs that come from the first 3 bones in the short plate of the cow's rib, before they are cut into smaller portions. If your butcher sells short ribs, talk with them about getting a few pieces before they are portioned into smaller short rib portions.

EDIBLE GLITTER is food-grade glitter made of sugars, corn starch, gum arabic, and pigments. Do not replace this ingredient with glitter used for arts and crafts; that is not safe to eat. Make sure the brand you are using is approved and safe for human consumption.

ELK STEW MEAT is meat from the shoulder and neck area of an elk. This meat is typically tougher and should be slow cooked in order to make it tender. Substitutes include any red meat used for stews, such as venison and beef chuck.

FENNEL is a vegetable and part of the parsley family. It has a mild licorice (anise) flavor and can be consumed raw or cooked. The bulb of the fennel is the typical part used for consumption, and the stalks work well for broths and flavoring. Celery can work as a substitute for fennel.

FENNEL SEEDS are seeds from the fennel plant's flowers that are dried. They have a sweet, licorice (anise) flavor that pairs well with savory dishes, especially pork dishes. Anise seed can be used as a substitute for fennel seeds, but make sure to use less because anise seed is much more pungent.

FENUGREEK SEEDS are a sweet and nutty-flavored spice. To substitute fenugreek flavor, you will need to use a combination of a small amount of maple syrup (for the sweetness) and mustard powder (for the bitterness). Another option is garam masala, which typically has fenugreek in the mixture.

FETA CHEESE is soft, salty, and brined cheese made from sheep's milk. It can be easily crumbled because of its soft texture. A substitute for feta cheese would be cotija cheese.

FISH SAUCE is a sweet, salty, pungent liquid that is made from fermented anchovies and salt. The salt content in this product is pretty high, and it can be used as a salt substitute to add an extra layer of umami. Be careful to not add too much of this product because it can easily overpower a dish. Fish sauce can be stored in the pantry for 2 to 3 years.

FURIKAKE is a dried seasoning used in Japanese cuisine for rice. It typically includes bonito flakes, seaweed, sesame seeds, sugar, and salt. It comes in many varieties like wasabi furikake, shiso furikake, etc. Furikake can be stored in the pantry for 1 year.

GIM see NORI (page 221)

GINGER BEER is a non-alcoholic, sweet, carbonated drink made from a fermentation process of ginger, sugar, and yeast. It can be substituted with ginger ale in a pinch, but ginger ale has a less intense flavor.

GLUTINOUS RICE FLOUR is sweet rice ground into a flour. Rice flour not labeled as glutinous is made from non-sweet rice. In Japanese cuisine, there are two kinds of glutinous rice flour: mochiko and shiratamako. Mochiko has the consistency of flour while shiratamako consists of large coarse granules.

GOAT STEW MEAT is meat from the shoulder of a goat. This meat is typically tougher and should be slow cooked in order to make it tender. Substitutes for this would be lamb shoulder.

GOAT CHEESE, also known as chèvre, is a soft cheese with a tangy flavor. Substitutes for goat cheese can vary depending on its use: For sauces, cream cheese works well, while feta cheese works well as a crumbling option.

GOCHUGARU is dried and ground Korean chili peppers.

GOCHUJANG is a thick Korean chili paste that contains red chili peppers, sticky rice, fermented soybeans, and sweeteners. Heat levels of gochujang can vary and are displayed on the container. Once gochujang is opened, it must be stored in an airtight container in the refrigerator.

GORGONZOLA is a type of soft, crumbly blue cheese. Its flavors are buttery and pungent. It is highly recommended to not substitute this ingredient but if unable to acquire this item, another variety of blue cheese can be used.

GREEK YOGURT is a yogurt where the whey has been removed by straining it out of regular yogurt. This changes the texture of the yogurt to be thicker and the flavor is more tangy. Greek yogurt can be substituted with plain yogurt.

GREEN PEPPERCORNS are peppercorns that have been harvested before they ripen. For the recipes using the green peppercorns in this book, you will want to purchase brined green peppercorns.

HEARTS OF PALM are the cores of several types of palm trees. These can be enjoyed raw or cooked.

HOISIN SAUCE is a sweet, thick sauce used in Chinese cuisine, especially barbeque, made from fermented soybean and Chinese five spice. It can be used for cooking or just as a dipping sauce. Hoisin sauce can be stored in the pantry until opened. Once opened, store in a refrigerator.

HORSERADISH is a very sharp, pungent root. It can be bought as a root that can be grated, or as an already grated product in a jar that should be stored in the refrigerator. It can be substituted with wasabi or mustard powder.

ICHIMI TOGARASHI is a single chili pepper flavor spice used in Japanese cuisine. Ichimi togarashi can be stored in the pantry. It can be replaced with any ground chili pepper of your liking.

IKURA (OR TARAKO) is salmon roe typically served raw. It must be stored in the refrigerator for no longer than 3 to 4 days.

JALAPENO is a green, medium chili pepper. It has a Scoville rating between 2000 and 8000 SHU. This can be replaced with another chili of your choice with a similar heat level, but keep in mind the flavor will be slightly different.

JAPANESE MAYO is a style of mayo using only egg yolks, several vinegars including rice and apple cider, and MSG. This mayo has a much richer egg flavor that is balanced by the variety of vinegars to give it a bit of a sweetness. It can be substituted with regular mayo and a small amount of rice vinegar, but the taste will be decently different.

JAPANESE WHISKY is a style of malted barley whisky developed in Japan that is heavily inspired by Scotch from Scotland. Any light whiskies from Scotland will work as a substitute.

JUNIPER BERRIES are the small, tart, piney-flavored seed cones of juniper trees. They can be cooked whole or crushed into a fine ground mixture. Juniper berries pair extremely well with wild game meat.

KALA NAMAK, also known as black Himalayan salt, is a pungent, sulfur-smelling rock salt. The ground version is pale pink in coloring. This can be stored in an airtight container in a cool pantry.

KASHMIRI CHILI POWDER is made from the kashmiri chili that has been dried and ground. Kashmiri chili has a mild heat with a vibrant red coloring. Good substitutes for kashmiri chili powder include paprika and other mild chilies.

KALAMATA OLIVES are dark brown olives originating from Kalamata, Greece. They have a milder taste than a black olive and are generally much sweeter and fruitier. Kalamata olives can be substituted for black olives, Nicoise olives, or Gaeta olives.

KIMCHI is a spicy fermented Korean vegetable dish. It is prepared with a brine and spices, similar to a pickling process. Napa cabbage is the most common vegetable for kimchi, but many kinds of vegetables can be fermented into kimchi. Kimchi must be stored in the refrigerator and occasionally opened to allow pressure from the fermentation to be released.

KING OYSTER MUSHROOMS, also known as king trumpet mushrooms, are large with thick, meaty stems. They have an earthy, woody taste with a texture close to scallops when cooked. These mushrooms can make great replacements for meat and seafood in dishes.

KIRSCH is a clear, infused alcohol made from sour cherries. It is not overly sweet. Kirsch can be substituted with cherry juice, apple juice, or another fruit brandy.

KOMBU is a type of dried kelp. Kombu can be used to enhance the flavors of stocks. It can be stored in a cool pantry.

LAMB MEAT comes from a young domesticated sheep, typically around 1 year old. This is different from mutton meat, which comes from an adult sheep, typically around 2 to 3 years old. Mutton typically contains more fat and the meat is a bit denser. If using mutton as a substitute for lamb, make sure to allow for a slightly longer cook time.

LION'S MANE MUSHROOMS are a large fungus with a fuzzy exterior, similar to a lion's mane. They are juicy and have a seafood-like taste. These mushrooms can make great replacements for meat and seafood in dishes.

LIQUID SMOKE is a flavoring liquid that will add the flavor of smoke when used.

MASCARPONE is a mild-flavored, soft, spreadable cheese. It is made from heavy cream and citric acid. Substitutes for mascarpone include crème fraîche, clotted cream, and cream cheese.

MERINGUE POWDER is dried, finely ground egg whites used to help stabilize frostings and icings.

MIDORI is a bright green, sweet, melon-flavored liqueur. Substitutes for Midori include other melon liqueurs and melon juice.

MILLET is a gluten-free seed that can be prepared as is or ground into flour. It has a slightly sweet flavor similar to corn. Substitutes for millet include bulgur and quinoa.

MINT is an herb with thin stems and ridged leaves. It has a sweet, cool flavor to it. This ingredient can be found as a fresh herb.

MISO is a paste made from fermented soybeans. Miso comes in several varieties, including shiro (white, the mildest flavor) and aka (red, allowed to age for longer, making it saltier and with a stronger flavor). Miso can be stored in an airtight container in the refrigerator.

MIZUNA is a leafy green vegetable with a mild pepper-like flavor. It can be eaten raw or cooked. Mizuna can be stored in a refrigerator for up to 5 days before it begins to wilt.

MOZZARELLA is a milk-flavored cheese. Two major varieties exist: fresh mozzarella and low-moisture mozzarella. Fresh mozzarella is a soft cheese with a delicate flavor, typically stored in liquid to keep it fresh. Low-moisture mozzarella is a dry variety that can easily be shredded. Recipes in this book use the low-moisture variety unless stated otherwise. Substitutes for low-moisture mozzarella include provolone, gouda, and fontina.

NARUTOMAKI is a type of kamaboko, Japanese fish cakes typically made from white fish. This variety usually features a pink spiral with a white exterior. Narutomaki should be stored in a freezer or refrigerator. If frozen, make sure to defrost before cooking with it.

NEGI is a Japanese variety of the Welsh onion. It has a similar taste profile to scallions but is larger and has a larger portion of the white stem on it. Negi can be substituted with scallions.

NIBOSHI are dried young sardines. They can be enjoyed as a snack or used for seasoning stocks.

NIGORI SAKE is a style of sake, an alcohol made from rice, that is known for its cloudy appearance. Typically, sake is filtered to remove all the rice grain solids after it has gone through the fermentation process. Nigori sake is filtered using a wider mesh strainer, allowing the fine rice grains to pass through. Note that when purchasing nigori sake, the fine rice grains will settle to the bottom of the bottle and should be shaken to combine.

NORI, also called gim, is the Japanese name for a dried, edible sheet of seaweed. It most commonly is used to wrap sushi rolls. Nori can be stored in a cool pantry.

OAT BRAN is the outer layer of the oat groat. Oat bran contains a higher amount of fiber and antioxidants than rolled oats. Substitutes for oat bran include wheat bran and rice bran.

OREGANO is a variety of herb with a stem that contains many tiny leaves. This ingredient can be found as a fresh herb or as dried and jarred leaves. Varieties include Greek oregano and Mexican oregano, which have unique flavor profiles and should not be interchanged. The recipes in this book used dry Greek oregano unless otherwise stated.

OYSTER MUSHROOMS are a cluster of small, thin-capped mushrooms. They have a mild flavor that is less earthy when compared with other mushrooms.

PALM SUGAR is a sweetener made from nectar of the coconut or palm flowers. Palm sugar can be substituted with brown sugar.

PANEER is a mild, non-melting, fresh cheese. It is made by curdling milk with acid, which gives it its non-melting characteristic. Substitutes for paneer include any other non-melting cheese and extra firm tofu.

PARSLEY is a fresh leaf herb with an herbal, bitter taste. There are several varieties with varying levels of flavor intensity. Any variety of parsley can be used for recipes in this book.

PARSNIP is an off-white root vegetable. It has a similar sweet flavor to carrots with heavy earthy undertones. Substitutes for parsnips include turnips, celery root, and carrots.

PEANUT OIL is a cooking oil made from peanuts. It is used for deep-frying because it has a high smoke point of roughly 450°F (232°C). Peanut oil can be substituted for any neutral oil with a similar smoke point, like canola or vegetable oil.

PEARLED BARLEY is barley that has been hulled and has had its bran layers removed. It has a very neutral flavor that is slightly nutty. Substitutes for pearled barley include bulgur and quinoa.

PLANTAINS are related to bananas but are much starchier and can't be eaten raw. Unripe plantains will be green in color. As they ripen, they turn yellow (medium) and eventually black (fully ripe).

POBLANO PEPPER is a large green chili pepper. It has a Scoville rating between 1000 and 2000 SHU. This can be replaced with another chili of your choice with a similar heat level, but keep in mind the flavor will be slightly different.

POPPY SEEDS are tiny, black seeds from the poppy plant. They have a nutty flavor. Substitutes for poppy seeds include toasted black sesame seeds and chia seeds.

PORK TENDERLOIN, also known as pork filet, is a long, thin cut of pork that runs along the spine. It is a very tender and lean piece of meat. This is a different cut compared to pork loin, which is much fattier and larger. For the recipes in this book, pork tenderloin can be swapped for pork loin, pork chop, or chicken breast. Keep in mind that cook time will vary.

PORCINI MUSHROOMS are large brown mushrooms with thick white stalks. This book uses dried porcini mushrooms, which should be rehydrated in warm water for 30 minutes before cooking.

POTATO STARCH is a fine powder made from extracting starches from potatoes. This ingredient is used to thicken items, similar to cornstarch. In most cases, cornstarch can be used as a substitute.

PUMPKIN PUREE is cooked pumpkin (typically sugar pumpkins) that has been mashed. This can be premade in a can, or a fresh pumpkin can be roasted until soft and then blended in a food processor until smooth. If using premade canned pumpkin, make sure to not use the pumpkin pie filling variety because it will contain spices.

PROVOLONE is a semi-hard cheese. The recipes in this book use the non-smoked variety of provolone cheese. Substitutes for provolone include fontina and mozzarella.

PU-ERH is a black tea that has been fermented after it has been dried. The flavor will vary based on the method of fermentation. It can range from bitter, vegetal to strong, smoky flavors. The recipes in this book use a ripened (shou) variety of pu-erh. It is highly recommended to not substitute this ingredient but if unable to acquire this item, use rich black tea.

QUESO ASADERO is a mild, semi-soft cheese used in Mexican cuisine. It has a very similar texture to string cheese and is used as a melting cheese. If queso asadero is difficult to find, it can be substituted with Monterey Jack or muenster cheese. Queso asadero should be stored in the refrigerator.

QUESO COTIJA is a hard, crumbly cheese used in Mexican cuisine. The cheese is traditionally aged, which gives it a salty flavor. If queso cotija is difficult to find, it can be substituted with feta cheese. Queso cotija can be stored in the refrigerator.

RED SNAPPER is a red-colored variety of white fish. It is a juicy fish with a slightly sweet, mild taste that pairs well with strong seasoning. Red snapper can be substituted with tilapia, grouper, or sea bass. Note that the cooking times will vary depending on the size of the fish.

REFRIED BEANS are pinto beans that have been boiled and then mashed into a paste. After being smashed, they are cooked again with seasoning. This ingredient can be found premade in the canned aisle near other beans.

ROBUSTA COFFEE is the second most popular type of coffee in the world (the most popular being arabica). Compared to arabica, it has more caffeine, less sugar, is easier to grow, and has a stronger bitter taste. Robusta is most often used in instant coffee and espresso blends.

ROSEMARY is an herb with thick woody stems that have many needle-like leaves. It has a piney, woodsy flavor to it. This ingredient can be found as a fresh herb or as leaves that have been dried and jarred.

RYE BERRIES are whole rye kernels with the hulls removed and no additional processing.

SAGE is a strong, warm-flavored herb with medium-sized oval leaves and tough stems. This ingredient can be found as a fresh herb or as dried and jarred leaves. When using the dry ingredient, make sure to not overdo it because it can overpower the dish.

SERRANO PEPPER is a small green chili pepper. It has a Scoville rating between 10,000 and 25,000 SHU. This can be replaced with another chili of your choice with a similar heat level, but keep in mind the flavor will be slightly different.

SESAME OIL is an oil made from sesame seeds. There are several varieties of sesame oil, and the recipes in this book use toasted sesame oil. Toasted sesame oil has a dark color and much stronger flavor profile than the raw variety. It is typically used as a finishing ingredient and not for cooking because the heat will reduce its flavor profile.

SHALLOT is a small variety of onion. It has a milder flavor than white onions and can often be used as a replacement for onions. This can be substituted with a sweet onion, leeks, or red onions.

SHIROAN is a fine, smooth, white bean paste. It can be stored in an airtight container in the refrigerator for up to 2 weeks.

SHIITAKE MUSHROOMS are mushrooms with small, tough stems and large caps that are dark brown in color. They have an earthy, smoky taste with a meaty texture.

SHOULDER BACON, or "European-style bacon," is is a style of bacon that has been prepared from the shoulder of the pig rather than the belly. This cut of bacon is typically much leaner and packs a stronger flavor punch than the belly variety. It can be substituted with any bacon variety.

SMOKED WHITEFISH is dry brined and smoked whitefish. Whitefish is a variety of freshwater fish (not to be confused with the term white fish, which refers to several varieties of fish). Substitutes for this ingredient include any smoked fish.

SOUR CREAM is a cream that has been fermented with a variety of lactic acid bacteria. This process results in a tangy, tart, and thick cream. It is recommended to not substitute this ingredient but if unable to acquire this item, Greek yogurt can be used instead.

SPIRULINA POWDER is an extract from spirulina, a microalga. For the recipes in this book, you will want to use the powder variety of this ingredient.

THYME is an herb with a cluster of stems that have many small leaves. It has a grassy, floral flavor to it. This ingredient can be found as a fresh herb or as leaves that have been dried and jarred.

TOBIKO is flying fish roe typically served raw. It must be stored in the refrigerator and can keep for up to 2 weeks.

TOMATO PASTE is a thick, concentrated tomato sauce that has been cooked for a long period of time, removing the water content. It is recommended to not substitute this ingredient but if unable to acquire this item, for every 1 tablespoon of tomato paste, replace with 3 tablespoons of tomato sauce.

TOMATILLOS are green, husk-covered fruit. They have a tart and subtly sweet flavor to them. When picking out tomatillos, make sure they are firm. It is highly recommended to not substitute this ingredient but if unable to acquire this item, green tomatoes can be used.

TONKATSU SAUCE is a thick, sweet sauce often accompanying fried dishes in Japanese cuisine. It can be stored in the pantry. Once opened, it can be stored in the refrigerator in an airtight container for about 2 months.

TURMERIC POWDER is dried, ground turmeric root. Turmeric is a bright orange-yellow rhizome that can be used in cooking. It has a bitter, earthy flavor similar to mustard and ginger.

UNSULFURED MOLASSES is a type of molasses that is made from ripened sugar cane without using sulfur dioxide as a preservative. It is highly recommended to not substitute this ingredient but if unable to acquire this item, dark corn syrup can work in a pinch.

VALERIAN ROOT is the root of the *Valeriana officinalis*, known for its relaxing capabilities. It has a pungent, woody flavor. When used for tea, it is dried and used just like any loose-leaf tea, mainly in blends.

WASABI is the stem of the *Wasabia japonica* plant, found in Japan. Authentic wasabi must be grated and served immediately to avoid losing its flavor and has a shelf life of 1 to 2 days at room temperature and 1 month in the refrigerator. More common is a wasabi substitute made of horseradish, mustard powder, and food coloring. This substitute is spicier and more pungent but can be stored in the refrigerator for up to 12 months.

WHEAT BERRIES are whole wheat kernels with the hulls removed and no additional processing.

WILD BOAR MEAT is a lean, slightly gamey meat from wild boars. Since these animals are much more active than domesticated pigs, the meat will typically cook quicker than regular pork. Wild boar meat can be substituted with the same cut of pork, but keep in mind the cook times will be different.

YUZU is a sour, tart citrus fruit grown primarily in East Asia. It is typically used for its juice and zest. Each fresh yuzu can yield about 2 to 3 teaspoons of juice. It might be difficult to find fresh yuzu, but juice and frozen zest might be easier to acquire. Yuzu can be substituted with another citrus fruit of your choice, such as a combination of lime and orange.

DIETARY RESTRICTIONS

Dietary and Personal Restrictions

Cooking is always a personal experience, and you should always feel comfortable replacing or removing any ingredients that you and your guests don't normally eat, for either personal or dietary reasons. Although you have a full experience of knowing what type of ingredients to avoid and replace, here are a few suggestions for some general dietary needs.

Adapting to Vegetarian Diets

Several recipes in this book are vegetarian- or vegan-friendly. Many recipes can be adapted to your dietary needs. Replace meat broths/stocks with vegetable broths/stocks. Swap out proteins with your favorite grilled vegetables or meat substitutes. This will affect the cooking times, so plan ahead.

Adapting to Gluten-Free Diets

For most recipes, you can use equal ratios of gluten substitute for flour, but be prepared to modify the quantity just in case the consistency seems off compared to how it is described in the recipes.

Adapting to Lactose-Free Diets

Feel free to replace milk and heavy cream with your favorite non-dairy milk. There are also plenty of alternatives to replace butter in recipes. I don't normally suggest replacing butter with oil because it doesn't give the same consistency needed for certain recipes. If you do use oil instead, approach it in smaller batches.

METRIC CONVERSIONS

VOLUME

U.S.	Metric
⅕ teaspoon (tsp)	1 ml
1 teaspoon (tsp)	5 ml
1 tablespoon (tbsp)	15 ml
1 fluid ounce (fl. oz.)	30 ml
⅕ cup	50 ml
¼ cup	60 ml
⅓ cup	80 ml
3.4 fluid ounces (fl. oz.)	100 ml
½ cup	120 ml
⅔ cup	160 ml
¾ cup	180 ml
1 cup	240 ml
1 pint (2 cups)	480 ml
1 quart (4 cups)	0.95 liter

TEMPERATURES

Fahrenheit	Celsius
200°F	93.3°C
212°F	100°C
250°F	120°C
275°F	135°C
300°F	150°C
325°F	165°C
350°F	177°C
400°F	205°C
450°F	233°C
475°F	245°C
500°F	260°C

WEIGHT

U.S.	Metric
0.5 ounce (oz.)	14 g
1 ounce (oz.)	28 g
¼ pound (lb.)	113 g
⅓ pound (lb.)	151 g
½ pound (lb.)	227 g
1 pound (lb.)	454 g

ABOUT THE AUTHORS

VICTORIA ROSENTHAL launched her blog, Pixelated Provisions, in 2012 to combine her lifelong passions for video games and food by recreating consumables found in many of her favorite games. When she isn't experimenting in the kitchen and dreaming up new recipes, she spends time with her husband and corgi hiking, playing video games, and enjoying the latest new restaurants. Victoria is also the author of *Fallout: The Vault Dweller's Official Cookbook*, *Destiny: The Official Cookbook*, *Street Fighter: The Official Street Food Cookbook*, and *The Ultimate FINAL FANTASY XIV Cookbook*. Feel free to say hello on social media at PixelatedVicka.

JENNA HELLAND is a writer and former principal designer for Wizards of the Coast. She was a world-builder on Magic: The Gathering sets from Shards of Alara to the Wilds of Eldraine. She is also the author of several novels, including *The August Five* and *Theros: Godsend*. She lives in the Pacific Northwest with her family.

Published by Titan Books, London, in 2023.

TITAN
BOOKS

A division of Titan Publishing Group Ltd
144 Southwark Street
London SE1 0UP
www.titanbooks.com

Find us on Facebook: www.facebook.com/TitanBooks

Follow us on Twitter: @titanbooks

All rights reserved.

Published by arrangement with Insight Editions, San Rafael, California, in 2023.

www.insighteditions.com

No part of this publication may be reproduced, stored in a retrieval system, or transmitted, in any form or by any means without the prior written permission of the publisher, nor be otherwise circulated in any form of binding or cover other than that in which it is published and without a similar condition being imposed on the subsequent purchaser.

A CIP catalogue record for this title is available from the British Library.

ISBN: 9781803367194

Publisher: Raoul Goff
VP, Co-Publisher: Vanessa Lopez
VP, Creative: Chrissy Kwasnik
VP, Manufacturing: Alix Nicholaeff
VP, Group Managing Editor: Vicki Jaeger
Publishing Director: Mike Degler
Art Director: Catherine San Juan
Design Manager: Megan Sinead Bingham
Senior Editor: Justin Eisinger
Editorial Assistant: Sami Alvarado
Managing Editor: Maria Spano
Senior Production Editor: Katie Rokakis
Production Associate: Deena Hashem
Senior Production Manager, Subsidiary Rights: Lina s Palma-Temena
Photography by Victoria Rosenthal

ROOTS of PEACE REPLANTED PAPER

Insight Editions, in association with Roots of Peace, will plant two trees for each tree used in the manufacturing of this book. Roots of Peace is an internationally renowned humanitarian organization dedicated to eradicating land mines worldwide and converting war-torn lands into productive farms and wildlife habitats. Roots of Peace will plant two million fruit and nut trees in Afghanistan and provide farmers there with the skills and support necessary for sustainable land use.

Manufactured in China

10 9 8 7 6 5 4 3 2 1